# IN HIS IMAGE
# IN HIS WORLD

# IN HIS IMAGE IN HIS WORLD

Edited by
**Eddie Tait**

CWR, 10 Brooklands Close,
Sunbury-on-Thames,
Middx TW16 7DX


**NATIONAL DISTRIBUTORS**
**Australia:** Christian Marketing Pty Ltd., PO Box 154,
North Geelong, Victoria 3215.
Tel: (052) 786100
**Canada:** Canadian Christian Distributors Inc.,
PO Box 550, Virgil, Ontario LOS 1TO.
Tel: 416 641 0631
**Republic of Ireland:** Merrion Press Ltd.,
10 D'Olier Street, Dublin.
Tel & Fax: 773316
**Malaysia:** Salvation Book Centre, (M) Sdn. Bhd.,
23 Jalan SS2/64, 47300 Petaling Jaya, Selangor
**New Zealand:** CWR (NZ), PO Box 4108,
Mount Maunganui 3030.
Tel: (075) 757412
**Singapore:** Alby Commercial Enterprises Pte Ltd.,
Garden Hotel, 14 Balmoral Road, Singapore 1025
**Southern Africa:** CWR (Southern Africa), PO Box 43,
Kenilworth 7745, South Africa.
Tel: (021) 7612560

Typeset by Watermark, Watford

Printed in Great Britain by Cox & Wyman Ltd., Reading

ISBN 1-85345-034-0

First published 1990

# CONTENTS

## SECTION 1

### The world

## SECTION 2

### The family

# SECTION 3

## The faith

# INTRODUCTION

*Government toppled ... Thousands dying in new famine outbreak ... Bereaved relatives sue disaster airline ...* These kind of images flash across our television screens daily, but where does the Christian stand in all this? How are we to react? Do we get our views from the TV, our daily newspaper, what our workmates say – or do we get them from the Bible?

There are lengthy books on the subjects available for those who have got the time to read them – but the majority haven't. Which is where *In His Image In His World* comes in. Its three sections will help you to grasp the essentials on issues affecting the world, the family and the Christian faith.

Don't get the idea that it's a comfortable armchair read, though. You'll find challenging Scriptures and challenging facts, as well as being faced with searching questions at the end of each day's study.

You probably won't agree with all we say, so we've included the sort of questions you will no doubt want to thrash out in your home group. You should find it a helpful guide to regular Bible study, as well as being valuable for church and Christian union study and discussion groups. Our prayer is that *In His Image In His World* will help you to learn more of what God is saying in these critical, but exciting days.

**Eddie Tait**

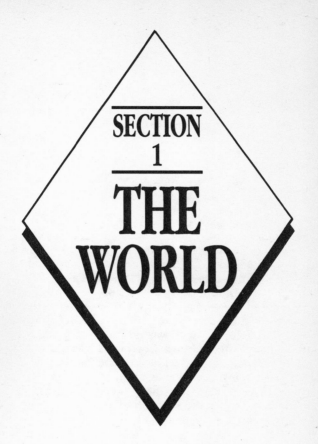

SECTION
1

THE
WORLD

# AT THE BEGINNING

## Monty White

*Dr A.J. Monty White was converted from atheism to Christianity while an undergraduate at the University College of Wales, Aberystwyth in 1964. He has written a number of books on creation and lectured and spoken on creation versus evolution in churches, schools, colleges and universities in the UK and Europe. Monty, his wife, Irene, and their three children live in Cardiff, where he is the Director of the International Office at the University of Wales. They attend Rhiwbina Baptist Church, where Monty leads a home Bible study group.*

### DAY 1

**Genesis 1:1 & 2; John 1:1–5**

The Scriptures start with God – the creator God. We cannot compare His capabilities with ours – He is unique! And His act of creation is unique. God, who has no beginning and has always existed, created all things. He was there at the beginning of time and even created time itself. Before time and the universe existed there was nothing but God. Not even empty space existed, yet the Lord God was there in all His glory. He dispelled the darkness of the "nothing" by creating the vast, empty universe, then created the beautiful planet Earth and made it so that it was fit for human habitation. He also created the sun, moon and stars to give us our day/night cycle and our seasons.

One of the problems in appreciating creation is that there is no analogy in modern experience to convey adequately what is meant by creation, for both Scripture and experience tell us that it has ceased. Creation starts with God, but the theory of evolution starts with man trying to bring everything neatly within the grasp of his finite mind. God created by saying, "Let there be" and instantaneously there was. Nowhere in Genesis chapter one do we read God saying, "Let there be these chemicals which, given the right conditions, may join together in such a way that, over a long period of time, there might evolve a living cell which might, by purely random processes operating over thousands of millions of years, evolve into such and such a creature."

Genesis teaches that all the plants and animals were created to reproduce their own kind rather than one type of creature being created to evolve into another type of creature. Fish, reptiles, birds and mammals were created as distinct types, but evolution teaches that fish evolved into amphibians which then evolved into reptiles, which then evolved into birds *and* animals.

The order of the events in the evolutionary hypothesis is also different from the creation story. Evolution says that marine organisms were the first life forms, whereas land plants come first in the creation account. Other differences are: fish before fruit trees, insects before birds, reptiles before whales, reptiles before birds according to evolution but vice-versa in each case in the Genesis account of creation. (Insects and reptiles are translated "things that move along the ground" in the NIV and "creeping things" in the Authorised Version). Struggle and death, according to evolutionists, were necessary prerequisites for man's biological progress, whereas the Bible declares that man himself was the cause of sin and death.

 **Lord God, thank you for being unique, all-powerful and for creating everything, including beautiful planet Earth for us to live upon. Help us to use wisely the resources you have put on this planet.**

 *With what or whom can we compare God?*

*Why does the theory of evolution detract from God's power and glory?*

**Genesis 2:1–3; Exodus 20:8–11**

God reveals His strength, power and glory in creation – and in how long He took to create everything. The Bible tells us that He completed the work in six days, literal days because the usual meaning of the Hebrew word *yom* which is translated *day* in Genesis chapter one is a literal day. And the numeral adjective (first, second, third...) indicates that they

11

they are literal days.

The Hebrew expression "evening and morning" defines the length and meaning of the day for us. The phrase also occurs in Daniel 8:14 & 26, where it clearly means *day*. Another important key is that the creation week is used as the basis of the six work days and one rest day of the fourth commandment. From this commandment alone it can be seen that the creation days were literal.

Some people would argue that the word *day* in Genesis chapter 1 means a long period of time, usually pointing to Psalm 90:4 and 2 Peter 3:8, where a day is compared to a thousand years. But both verses are simply figures of speech to show that God is not constrained by the same time parameters as we humans are.

God is no longer creating, for the six days of creation are past. Nor is He resting, for the seventh day has also gone. The Bible, however, clearly teaches that God is now very active in His creation (Col. 1:17) and also in our lives (Ps. 121:1–8).

 **Lord God, thank you for giving us the weekly cycle, for still upholding creation and for watching over me. Help me to continually live in the wonder of your majestic power and give you the worship that is due to you.**

 *How much time do you devote to the Lord?*

*What other things do you think God is doing at the moment?*

**Genesis 1:14–23; Psalm 19:1**

God's glory, strength, power and majesty can be seen in the number of stars in the universe. Astronomers tell us that our sun is a star and that it belongs to our galaxy, which we call the Milky Way. There are about a hundred thousand million stars in the Milky Way, but it's not the only galaxy – there are about a hundred thousand million of them in the universe! There are as many galaxies in the universe as there are stars in a galaxy.

So the total number of stars in the whole universe is mind blowing! About a hundred thousand million multiplied by a hundred thousand million. That's about $10^{22}$ – 10,000,000,000,000,000,000,000. The number is so large that if you counted up to three million *every second*, then it would take you over a hundred million years to count up to this staggering number!

The opening chapter of Genesis tells us that God made *all* the stars – 10,000,000,000,000,000,000,000 of them. And He made them in an instant! He spoke – and they were there. Furthermore, in Psalm 147:4 we see that He calls all the stars by name – all 10,000,000,000,000,000,000,000 of them. No wonder we read in the next verse that God is great and His understanding has no limit.

Considering the creation of the stars should make us realise what a powerful and mighty God we have. No wonder we can cast our burdens on Him and sing that nothing is too difficult for Him to do!

 **Almighty God, thank you for the stars which you have created and which remind us of your power and greatness. Thank you, too, for the Morning Star and that He has shone in our hearts.**

 *Why did God create so many stars?*

*Who is the Morning Star?*

 **Genesis 1:26–28; 2:7,18–25**

Although God used material He had created to make Adam (the dust of the ground), the first human being was not the result of an evolutionary process. Having made him physically, God then breathed life into Adam so that he became a living soul – made in God's image, with a body, soul and spirit.

Eve, too, was not the product of chance natural processes, but was created by Almighty God using part of Adam's side. Eve was made as a companion to Adam – made from his side to show that woman's true position is by the side of her husband, helping and supporting him. She was also made that way to show how men should treat women: as their equals.

The creating of Adam and Eve is in direct contradiction to evolutionist theory that humans descended from ape-like creatures. There is no evidence in fossil findings that half-human/half-ape creatures ever existed. There *have* been cases of mistaken identity (such as when a pig's tooth was taken to be that of a hypothetical ape-man), and of deception (the Piltdown man saga being a prime case). Popular images portrayed in children's books and museum reconstructions of ape-people are no more than the figments of imagination.

Scientific evidence from the fields of anatomy, biochemistry and genetics strongly supports the idea that humans have been *designed* – and that this design must have been by a mighty and powerful God. Therefore we have every reason to say, with king David, that we are fearfully and wonderfully made (Ps. 139:14).

 **Thank you, Lord God, for creating men and women. Thank you for our companions. Help us to treat our friends and relatives as you would have us treat them.**

 *What does Scripture mean by the statement that men and women are created in God's image?*

*What does the creation of Adam and Eve teach us about the relationships that should exist between men and women?*

**DAY 5**

**Genesis 2:16 & 17; 3:1–24**

When God looked at everything He had made, He saw that it was "very good," Genesis 1:31 tells us. This is in stark contrast to the apostle Paul's statement, "For we know that the whole creation has been groaning as in the pains of childbirth right up to the present time" (Rom. 8:22). The dramatic change had come through rebellion against God – Adam and Eve had eaten the forbidden fruit from the tree of knowledge of good and evil.

Satan, in the guise of a serpent, tempted Eve into disobedience by sowing seeds of doubt in her mind about God's command to her and her husband. He also lied to her by declaring that she would not die if she ate the forbidden fruit which, incidentally, was not the apple of popular myth. Confusion has arisen because the Latin word for evil is *malus* and the word is also translated *apple*. Because malus appeared in the Latin Vulgate Bible in the phrase "tree of good and evil," people began to think of an apple tree when they read this phrase.

As soon as Adam and Eve ate the fruit, they began to die physically (Gen. 3:19; 5:5). We die because Adam sinned (1 Cor. 15:21,22). But more important than dying physically is spiritual death. Adam and Eve suffered this immediately — they were separated from God (Gen. 3:8).

Adam and Eve's sin set off a chain reaction among mankind which has continued down the ages. Man has an awareness of God but, because of his rebellion, he leaps at any chance to deny God's existence, choosing to live without reference to Him. Man is dead in his "transgressions and sins" (Eph. 2:1) and the only way to come alive is to repent and receive forgiveness through Jesus Christ.

 Help us not to sin, Lord Jesus, but to obey your commands. May we not be beguiled by those who would try to sow doubts in our minds about living your way.

 *Why do we find it easier to sin than to obey God?*

*Why do people need to be born again?*

 **Revelation 21:1, 5–8, 22–27**

God originally made man and woman in His own image and glory (1 Cor. 11:7), but because of sin we fall short of this (Rom. 3:23). We will only be restored when the work of redemption is complete and we once again reflect God's glory (Rom. 8:19–21,29,30; 2 Cor. 3:18; Rom. 5:1,2). This restoration can only be achieved in and through the Lord Jesus Christ (Gal. 4:4,5; 1 Pet. 2:24; 1 John 1:7).

The new creation began with salvation and will be complete when God makes all things new, as the first verse of today's passage tells us. Peter tells us to keep this in mind (2 Pet. 3:9–14).

The redeemed are described as God's new creation (2

Cor. 5:17). Full restoration of the original creation has yet
to take place, although Christians have been given the down
payment (*earnest*, AV) of it (Eph. 1:14). Regeneration by
the Holy Spirit (Tit. 3:5), which the Christian experiences at
conversion, is a foretaste of the regeneration that will occur
when the Lord Jesus Christ returns (Matt. 19:28).

When Christ returns we will be restored to our former
glory and be as God intended us to be in the beginning – just
as Adam and Eve were before the fall. The physical creation
will only be restored to its former glory when God creates a
new heaven and a new earth. Then, and only then, will the
visions of Isaiah 11:6–9 and Habakkuk 2:14 be fulfilled.

 **Thank you, Lord, that we are new creatures in Christ
because of what you have done at Calvary. Thank you,
too, that this reminds us that you are restoring your creation and that one day we will be perfectly restored in
you.**

 *When will we be perfect?*

*What is your attitude to those who have not even experienced
the foretaste of complete restoration to the image of God?*

 **Genesis 1:1–2:3**

God is the Creator and there is no hint in Scripture that He used evolutionary processes when
He created. The creation reflects His greatness
and glory. God created the beautiful planet
Earth and made all the plants and animals to live on it in
perfect union. He also created people – in perfect union
with creation and with God. But all this was spoiled by
Adam's deliberate disobedience.

Yet God did not forsake His creation, for He is still
actively involved in it. He sent His only begotten son, Jesus
Christ, into this world to live a perfect, sinless life and
become sin for us through death on Calvary's cross. When
we accept this redemptive, sacrificial death on our behalf,
we are born again through the Holy Spirit and become
God's new creation.

The creation will finally be restored at the return of the

Lord Jesus Christ. At that time Christians will be fully restored to the glory that Adam and Eve had before the fall. Then, and only then, will we be perfect. God will also at that time create a new heaven and a new earth.

This view of our future is so different from that held by evolutionary scientists, who have to rely on uniformitarian philosophy in order to look at the future. This philosophy states that the present is the key to the past as well as the future. The apostle Peter warns his readers about this philosophy in his second letter by saying that people who scoff at the promise of the Lord's coming do so because they are ignorant of God's ways. Christians, on the other hand, can be sure of the future. We have a hope that is steadfast and certain, for our hope is fixed on God the Creator, Saviour and coming King!

 Thank you, Lord, for being our creator, for being involved in the physical creation. Thank you, Lord Jesus, for being our Saviour and that one day you are coming again, that there will be a new heaven and a new earth, and that the whole creation will be perfectly restored.

---

**FOR GROUP DISCUSSION**

● What questions are you asked when discussing the creation with non-believers?

● Why should the early chapters of Genesis be taken literally?

● Are scientists to be absolutely trusted when they tell us their discoveries about our origins?

● What effect has sin had on the creation in general and on humankind in particular?

● What are the differences between the Biblical view of the future and that of evolutionary scientists?

● Are you excited about the promised return of the Lord Jesus Christ?

---

**Suggested further reading**

*Bone of Contention* Sylvia Baker (Evangelical Press)
*Evolution and the Authority of the Bible* Nigel Cameron (Paternoster Press).
*Evolution: Challenge of the Fossil Record* Dr Duane Gish (CLP [Master Books])
*How Old is the Earth?* Dr A.J. Monty White (Evangelical Press)
*Scientific Case for Creation* Dr A.J. Monty White (Heath Christian Trust)
*Wonderfully Made* Dr A.J. Monty White (Evangelical Press).

# WHOSE EARTH IS IT, ANYWAY?

## Eddie Tait

*Eddie Tait is Editor of* Revival, *CWR's Prayer Chain magazine. A former provincial newspaper journalist, he and his Finnish-born wife, Barbro, whom he met when they were students at Elim Bible College, have three sons and are involved with Harrow International Christian Centre. A keen hillwalker, he first became concerned about environmental issues through seeing the spoiling of his favourite corner of England, the Lake District. He has also written the following two, interrelated, sections — on the Christian's attitude to politics and the question of world peace.*

## DAY 1

**Psalm 24:1; 104:1, 4–18, 24–26**

Green has become very popular. In the environmental sense, that is. So many people are seeing green that it's no longer considered to be a hippy-type fringe activity. World leaders have become greatly concerned about it and major political parties in the West, as well as the Greens, have adopted green policies. There's been a great awakening of concern in recent times for the health of planet Earth. It's in desperately poor shape, having suffered years of appalling abuse and neglect.

Wars have laid lands waste. Deserts increase by some 50 million acres a year through over-cultivation and over-grazing, soils have been robbed of their nutrients. About 18 million acres of forest are destroyed annually. The Amazon rain forests, containing rich, natural resources, are being systematically devastated by greedy men seeking fortunes out of ranching. Topsoil erosion means that getting on for 20 million acres of valuable crop land is lost each year. Industrial pollution has affected thousands of lakes, especially in Scandinavia, killing fish and other forms of life.

There's the greenhouse effect – the raising of the temperature in the earth's atmosphere through burning forest and spewing out industrial pollution. And there's the huge hole in the ozone layer over Antarctica, which has been linked with significant increases of skin cancer cases.

No wonder alarm is reverberating around the world! It's an issue that should concern Christians, with the proviso that it is from the right base – that the earth is God's, not ours. It has gone wrong because man has assumed that it is his to do what he likes with, rather than looking after what God has made.

 **Father God, when I consider what man has done to the beautiful earth you have created, I am appalled. Help me to do my part in looking after it.**

 *What has struck you most about the Scriptures you have read today?*

*How does the realisation that the earth belongs to God affect your attitude to what mankind has been doing to it?*

 **Genesis 1:26–30; 2:8–18**

A Christian's approach to environmental issues starts from a different premise to the rest of society: that he has been appointed to be a steward of God's earth, not its master. Man, instead of following the Maker's instructions, has gone his own way and, in seeking to satisfy his never-ending greed and lust, has exploited and spoiled a once-beautiful planet. One striking example of this is the Chernobyl disaster. Three years after the nuclear power plant near Kiev leaked and blew up, the levels of radiation were still so high that a village 300 km away had to be abandoned. Many people are still suffering as a result of the gas explosion which destroyed the American Union Carbide company's chemical plant in Bhopal, India. Not only did thousands lose their lives, but survivors were blinded, badly burned, and left with serious breathing difficulties and damaged kidneys.

God's command to man to "subdue" the earth was not a blank cheque for unlimited exploitation, but responsible management and service. Adam and all who came after him, including you and me, were to organise and utilise the creation for man's benefit and God's glory (Rev. 4:11). The present state of the earth reflects man's sin against God and, while we Christians can, and must, share some of the concerns expressed by environmental pressure groups, we do so for a different motive – to please God rather than for self-preservation.

Because we acknowledge that nature belongs to God and mankind holds it in trust, we must guard against seeking humanistic utopias which imply that greater understanding and progress will lead to solving all the problems. Such philosophies exclude the Creator and His indispensable activity.

We must also be careful, in our stewardship, to worship the Creator, not the created. Saving the whale or being vegetarian is almost a religion to some people!

 **Thank you, dear Lord, that you have made me a steward to look after your world, this planet Earth. Help me to discharge my duties properly, always glorifying you.**

 *Is your motive for improving the environment in line with God's?*

*What is the Lord challenging you to do as a result of today's reading?*

 **Luke 12:16–31**

Was Jesus an environmentalist? Maybe not directly so, but His understanding and care for the ecology is certainly implied by His frequent illustrations from agriculture and nature. The parable of the rich fool (vv. 13–21) is a striking illustration of His perception of man's greed and exploitation of God-given resources for selfish ends.

"The good life" philosophy abounds in Western culture today. Millions starve in India, Ethiopia and other parts of the world while people in rich countries with abundant harvests make noises about the situation, momentarily stop to write a cheque for a few pounds in response to an appeal and then, with their consciences satisfied, carry on with their affluent lifestyles. Around 40,000 children in the Third World die of starvation each year while Britain alone has a grain mountain of around four million tons – costing millions of pounds each year to store.

God provides food and clothes through the earth's resources to meet our needs (Gen. 9:2&3, Good News Bible), not for our over-indulgence. The problem with today's luxuries is that they become tomorrow's necessities. This has resulted in more and more cattle in areas such as Central America being fattened with more and more feed to meet the bigger and bigger demands of Western nations for beef and yet more beef. Millions of kangaroos have been killed legally and illegally in Australia for a wide range of products including handbags, sports shoes and pet food.

Jesus' reference to birds, grass and flowers emphasises His Father's concern for all creation. Man's greed, in contrast, has resulted in the extinction of so many species of plant-life and animals, and driven many other creatures from their natural habitats through clearing forests to graze cattle and introduce more and more intensive crop-growing to meet his insatiable demands.

 **Thank you, Lord, for the food I have to eat each day and the clothes I have to wear. Help me not to crave for luxuries, but thirst for your righteousness.**

 *What can you do without in the way of food and clothes which would reflect your commitment to being God's steward?*

*What have you got that will be of benefit to someone else?*

### DAY 4

**Matthew 10:29–31; Psalm 8:1–9; 139:13–16**

Although Jesus reveals His concern and care for birds and plants, it is in the context of His *greater* care for human beings. Man is top of God's creation tree! So concern for the environment which ignores the plight of suffering men, women and children is wide of the mark indeed.

While environmental pressure groups campaign – rightly so – against the killing of the whales, generally they ignore the slaughter of millions of unborn children through abortion! Repeal of the 1967 Abortion Act should be high on our list as far as British stewards of creation are concerned! As we went to press, whether or not to use RU486 in our land was in the news – the do-it-quietly French abortion pill. Nationwide usage of it would result in an even bigger killing rate of unborn children.

And what about the Soviet Union? The average woman there has between six and eight abortions, with over six million children being killed off in the womb each year.

As if that is not enough, add the millions of human beings who are suffering as a result of war, displacement from their homelands and living amidst appalling deprivation in refugee camps. Because God was concerned above all else for the crown of His creation, so should we be.

 **Oh Father, how my heart weeps over man's callousness, especially to other human beings. Use me in opening other's eyes to inhuman, destructive practices such as the killing of unborn children and herding people away from their homelands like cattle.**

 *Have you ever written to your local MP about the need to change the Abortion Act and stop the killing of innocent, unborn children?*

*Who and which country benefits most from killing whales? What is the main motive? Check it out and pray about it.*

 **Genesis 9:8–17; Ephesians 1:9–12; Colossians 1:15–20; Romans 8:19–25**

While sharing society's concern about Earth's desperate state, the Christian differs markedly on the ultimate solution, for this planet's destiny is in God's hands, not ours. And God's promise is that the whole of creation will one day be restored to its former perfection. Our passages show that created nature is Christ's and that His death on Calvary's Cross not only brought reconciliation of man to God, but to nature as well.

This, in turn, points to man's authority over nature and his responsibility to God for it. Although fundamentally the

Good News is a call for sinful men, women and children to repent and receive Christ as Saviour and Lord, it is also a promise of redemption for all creation (Mark 16:15).

So although Christians share the concerns of society about the state of the earth and desire for governments to take the necessary action to stop the industrial pollution that's poisoning the atmosphere and killing fish, seals and trees, as well as the dumping of toxic waste, we can lift up our heads in hope. For we know that, one day, we and all creation will be restored to God's original perfection.

A truly Christian view of environmental problems contains not only concern but realistic optimism. A believer is, in Christ, the first fruits of God's redemptive purposes for nature – and can eagerly look forward to total fulfilment.

 **Thank you, Lord Jesus, that you not only redeemed me on the Cross, but that one day all creation will be restored to its former glory.**

 *How does the knowledge that Christ's redemptive work is for all of creation affect your attitude to the present state of the environment?*

*How will it affect your sharing of the Good News with others?*

 **Psalm 104:1–31; 23:1–3**

At 2,000 feet we hit snow. From then on it was a struggle to the ridge, even with proper boots on. But eventually, we arrived at the top of Red Pike, our first summit of the day. Later, as we continued along the ridge after reaching High Stile, the highest point on the walk, I paused and marvelled at it all. We were standing above the clouds, which obscured Buttermere completely. Above was clear, blue sunlit sky. My heart just sang praises to God!

A couple of hours later on that Easter-time afternoon, on the way down from High Crag, the third and last summit, my heart was welling up again with thankfulness to the Creator as my eyes took in the peaceful lake and pale sunlight highlighting gentle shades of green on the surrounding fells. Thankfulness to God for the beauty of the earth is an essential part of a Christian's attitude to the environment.

A summer later, on a fell top in the same area, I was lunching with my family in a large shelter of rough stones when my eyes were drawn to the heap of cans and other rubbish in the corner. It wasn't the only occasion, in the Lake District and in other parts of Britain, that I have come across man's lack of respect for the countryside. More ease of access to the wilder places has led to increased litter dropping and vandalism, such as hills being scarred by many boots making short cuts instead of following the old zigzags. Soil erosion is now a major problem on the fells.

God not only made this earth for His pleasure and for supplying mankind with food, but for our enjoyment as well. As stewards, we need to set an example in big and small ways, like keeping to the footpaths – although that can be hard at times because of the increasing number of instances of farmers ploughing up paths or fencing off rights of way.

 **Lord God, I praise you for the beauty of the countryside and that you made it for us to enjoy. Help me to do my part in keeping it beautiful and unspoilt.**

 *Does the countryside give you cause to praise its Creator?*

*What do you think you can do to preserve the beauty of the rural areas?*

 **Matthew 5:14–16; James 3:17**

Man's exploitation of God's world has resulted in global environmental catastrophe. To him, quick profitability is paramount when it comes to using the earth's resources, rather than the long-term good of all. Take modern farming methods: Many pigs spend their lives chained to the floor in iron stalls, with hardly any room to move, instead of being free to roam in outside enclosures. Then there's battery hens – living in frustrating, overcrowded conditions in stacked cages, often suffering disease and injury until they are loaded into lorries for slaughter. Factory farming has no respect for creation, either in its treatment of animals and poultry while the creatures are alive or in the less than humane ways of killing them.

So facing up to environmental and conservation issues as a Christian means, largely, living by example. Here are a few ways we can do this:

☐ Use lead-free petrol – and conserve petrol when you can, such as turning off the ignition if you're well and truly stuck in a traffic jam. ☐ Use non-CFC household sprays (there are many on the market, now that the danger of chlorofluorocarbons to the ozone layer has been realised). ☐ Organic gardening, rather than using chemicals to spray flowers, fruit and vegetables. ☐ Reassess your food consumption, particularly the amount of meat you eat, and reduce if necessary. ☐ Examine your attitude to fashion – whether you allow it to dictate the frequency in which you buy new clothes or whether you buy only what is necessary. ☐ Use your cooker, washing machine, TV and the like for as long as you can keep them operating reliably, rather than giving in to the temptation to replace them with the latest models. ☐ Try to avoid buying items known to have been produced through exploitation of people or extreme cruelty to animals. ☐ Financially support a Christian environmental care project – Tear Fund (100 Church Road, Teddington, Middx. TW11 8QE) or World Vision (8 Abington Street, Northampton NN1 2BR) run them.

One question that arises is whether Christians should join environmental pressure groups. The answer really boils down to whether God is calling us to join so that we can influence and change them from within. The militant action of some is certainly not a Christian's way of campaigning for change. Environmental groups tend to embrace not just evolutionist, but New Age thinking, with its Hinduistic and other Eastern religious beliefs and practices. According to New Age, we have offended Mother Earth through abusing the environment, so we must acknowledge this and be reconciled to nature. New Age propagates the belief that a "deliverer" called Maitreya will come to protect the environment and bring about global unity, peace and harmony. All this, however, denies

Christ's work of reconciliation on the Cross and is also a direct contradiction to the Bible's statement that "The earth is the Lord's and everything in it."

 **Lord God, help me to be a shining example in my love and care for the earth you have created, for your glory.**

---

### FOR GROUP DISCUSSION

• In what ways have these studies on the environment altered your thinking on the issue?

• What do you think Christians should be doing to improve the environment?

• Should your church have a green policy?

• Look up Leviticus 25:1–7. What effect do you think a "sabbath of rest" every seventh year would have on modern Western farms if put into practice?

• Daniel refused to "defile himself with the royal food" – which no doubt included meat – and ate vegetables instead (Dan. 1:8–15). Does this mean Christians should be vegetarians?

• How can your church help people in other parts of the world who are being exploited?

• In what practical ways, other than suggested in these studies, can you reflect God's love and care for His creation?

---

### Suggested further reading

*The Earth in Our Hands* Roland Moss (Inter-Varsity Press)
*Tending the Garden* edited by Wesley Granberg-Michaelson (Eerdmans)
*Curriculum Unmasked* (chapter 1) Mark Roques (Monarch/Christians in Education).

# POLITICS AND POWER

## Eddie Tait

**DAY 1**

**Proverbs 8:15,16; Genesis 9:5 & 6; Psalm 82:1–8**

It must be one of the favourite British pastimes: moaning about the Government. What those in power have or have not done – and what, in our opinion, they should be doing. Yet whatever we think of our rulers, they are there because God put them there – and they govern for our good. They rule over us on His behalf.

Government was one of the key structures God introduced after Adam's sin and fall (Gen. 3:1-24) to restrain evil, preserve order and promote justice. Along with two other institutions, marriage and the family, it was to provide stability in society. Today, all three institutions are under such great attack, so can we wonder that the world is in such turmoil! When people rebel and seek to overthrow God's structures for the wellbeing of mankind, they sin against Him and the nation suffers as a result.

Our Genesis passage records the beginnings of government as, after the flood, people began to multiply again. It emphasises that primary function of maintaining law and order and punishing evildoers. Two chapters on, God intervened at Babel, confused the languages and scattered the peoples across the globe to form many nations and national governments (Gen. 11:1–8).

Rulers are warned by the Supreme Ruler of the dire consequences of unjust, power-hungry governing – inevitable judgment (Prov. 29:4; Amos 5:24). That judgment and deposing from power may seem a long time in coming to citizens suffering under a repressive regime, but it will surely come (Isa. 40:22,23). God raises up rulers and puts them down after using them to fulfil His sovereign purposes. Just as he raised up king Cyrus to overthrow the Babylonians and release the Jews from captivity and exile to go home and rebuild Jerusalem (Isa. 45:12, 13; 2 Chron. 36:22,23), so justice will come even to nations under the harshest of governments. The overthrow of Presidents Nicolae Ceausescu of Romania, Erick Honecker of East Germany, Gustav Husak of Czechoslovakia and Manuel Noriega of Panama all strikingly illustrate this fact.

 **Lord God, thank you for the government of my land. I'm grateful that it is there for my good and your purposes.**

 *Does the knowledge that God instituted national government change your attitude to those who rule your land?*

*Jot down ways you benefit through those who govern.*

 **Romans 13:1–14; 1 Peter 2:13–17; 1 Timothy 2:1, 2**

We Christians should be model citizens! For we know that God has put rulers over us for our good and social benefit. Such knowledge should affect our attitude to government ministers and everyone else in some kind of civil authority, including local government officials and the village policeman. We should not fiddle our taxes or evade paying duty on something we can easily slip through customs on our return from our package holiday or business trip.

While the apostle Paul warns of punishment at the hands of the authorities for wrongdoing, it should not be the fear of that which motivates us, but obedience to God, our love for Him and desire to serve Him through the witness of our lives. Disobedience to the State is disobedience to God himself.

We are commanded to respect and honour both the people who rule and the positions they hold. Even if a president or prime minister is intoxicated with power and a disgrace to that high position he or she has been entrusted with, we must still reverence the office they hold. Nothing is said about the form of government or its party political colour! In fact, both Paul and Peter penned these words while living under an occupying power, when Jews were fermenting rebellion against the Romans. Even behind the godless emperor Nero's brutal reign of terror God could be seen working His purposes out, especially in being the instrument of divine judgment against a God-rejecting people.

While Christians are to show exemplary behaviour towards the government of the day, we are not to be silent about injustice or blindly accept a ruler's actions when they are clearly against the law of God. And, in all situations, we are commanded to use one weapon in our dealings with the authorities — prayer. Intercession for rulers is the vital key for producing the right climate for peaceful living. In such a climate Christians are more able to carry out the task of bringing the message of salvation to needy mankind.

 **Lord, help me to be an exemplary citizen and show proper respect towards the authorities you have placed over me.**

 *Is there any attitude towards rulers which you need to put right?*

*When did you last pray for the Government?*

 **Matthew 22:15–22; Philippians 3:20, 21**

My wife wanted to become a British citizen. But to do so meant relinquishing citizenship of the land of her birth, Finland. While Britain recognised dual nationality, the Scandinavian country didn't. If she could have officially become British and stayed Finnish, she would actually have held triple citizenship, for as a Christian she also belongs to the Kingdom of God.

Dual citizenship creates tension for the Christian when the interests of both kingdoms clash — as they frequently do. Jesus recognised this and clearly defined the boundary beyond which the State must not intrude.

It all came out through a trap laid by the Pharisees. By asking Jesus whether it was right to pay the deeply resented Roman poll tax imposed upon every Jew, they expected him to say one of two things which would have got Him into deep trouble. "Yes" would be taken as supportive of the occupying power hated by so many Jews; "No" would be seen as rebellion against the rulers and therefore they could have Him arrested as a threat to the Romans. But Jesus responded by asking for a Roman denarius, the type of coin used to pay the tax. It had the emperor's head inscribed on it, a fact the Pharisees readily acknowledged. In one sentence Jesus demolished their scheming and left them speechless: "Give to Caesar what is Caesar's, and give to God what is God's."

Use of the denarius, to pay tax and buy things, was acknowledgement of the ruler's authority over the day-to-day economics of life. But there was something else on the coin, which throws light on Jesus also saying, "Give to God what is God's." Around the emperor's image was inscribed, "Tiberius Caesar Augustus, son of the divine Augustus." And literally on the other side of the coin was Tiberius' mother portrayed as the goddess of peace with the words, "highest priest." That was blasphemy – an exceeding of the State's authority. God and God alone is to be worshipped – not Caesar.

 **Thank you, Lord God, that you alone are worthy of my worship. Help me not to confuse the issue of obeying the State and serving you.**

 *What conflict have you experienced recently as a citizen of both an earthly kingdom and the Kingdom of God?*

*What do the implications of giving to Caesar what is Caesar's and giving to God what is God's mean personally to you?*

 **Daniel 3:1–30; Hebrews 11:16**

The departure point in choosing to obey God rather than the State comes when a ruler tries to make Christianity and Christian conscience subservient to himself and the political system he heads. That's what King Nebuchadnezzar had his idol built for. He was quite happy for other religions to exist – as long as they didn't take prime place.

When Christians put God first, even when it could mean losing their lives, no political system can stand against them and their Master. This has been proved all through history, from the first days of the Early Church right up to the Church of the late 20th century, especially in places like China where, despite the persecution and martyrdom during Mao Tse-tung's Cultural Revolution, the Church has grown to a staggering conservatively estimated 50 million strong.

Christians who refuse to compromise will always have a subversive effect on the world's ideologies. That's because true Christian faith is unique – distinct compared with any political or other religious systems. It refuses to owe any other allegiance but to Jesus Christ, its Head. The State may seek to find common ground in religious faith, but this is a non-negotiable area for Christians. Our stand is on God's Word alone.

Daniel and his friends held high positions in King Nebuchadnezzar's administration (Dan. 2:48,49), but position meant nothing when it came to a choice between bowing to the king or to God. They were marching to a higher drumbeat than Nebuchadnezzar's self-promoting one – for they knew they belonged to an everlasting kingdom rather than a frail, man-built one which shifted on the sands of relative values. In standing for God and refusing to compromise even when staring death in the face, they opened up the way for God to move in miraculous power – and political change.

 Lord God, thank you that you are greater than any political system. Help me to serve you above all else and not compromise in my stand for you.

 *Is there any compromise in your life which hinders your relationship with God?*

*Does your life have a positively subversive effect on others?*

**DAY 5**

**Daniel 6:1–28**

Kings and queens, emperors, presidents, prime ministers and dictators have sought, down the centuries, to build lasting kingdoms. Many of them, like Nebuchadnezzar and Darius, have tried to unite their kingdom under one religion – an amalgam of all faiths. In some countries today, church groups have become subservient to the State, seeking merely to survive on what the regime allows it to do rather than taking an unashamed stand on Biblical truth. Many have embraced the so-called *liberation theology,* which is Marxist-based and sees salvation as the overthrow of political oppression. This is rife in Central America, but it is also infiltrating into Western churches.

There's an intense struggle going on to find common ground among the various religions, hence the rise of interfaith gatherings, which are contrary to Scripture (John 14:6). Once Christians fall for this, they get sucked into a form of religion which is devoid of spiritual power (2 Tim. 3:5).

Daniel must have been subjected to many temptations in high political office to compromise his faith, to let his standards slip. His honesty, integrity, righteousness and sense of justice were such a threat to his self-seeking, sensual colleagues that they decided to have him removed. So another test of loyalty had to be faced. King Darius, though open to God, feared for his political life – and his head. Weakly, he followed the party line, for the temptations and trappings of power were too much for him.

But Daniel was unmoved. When he heard of the king's decree to worship the king instead of the King of kings, he went back home and prayed to God, "just as he had done before" (v. 10). The daily discipline of prayer, plus study of the Scriptures, are foundational to steadfast, uncompromising Christianity. By facing Jerusalem to pray, Daniel was emphasising his allegiance to the Kingdom of God. That was the place which shaped his character – not Babylon. And Daniel again found that God was with him – even in the lions' den. What an effect one man completely sold out to God had on the political structures of his day!

 **Lord, help me to be disciplined in prayer and faithful to your Word – a Christian who doesn't compromise.**

*How do you think you would react if faced with the same choice as Daniel?*

*How disciplined is your prayer life?*

 **Acts 4:1–31**

Civil authorities cross into forbidden territory when they try to stop Christians evangelising. Such attempts to stop the spread of the Gospel has been going on since the beginning of the Early Church after Pentecost and the principle for Christ's followers is the same – disobedience to earthly rulers and obedience to God, whatever the cost. If Peter and John had not made their stand when arrested and forbidden to "speak no longer to anyone in this (Jesus') name", the infant Church would probably have died there and then.

Instead, their fearless stand left a principle and an example which has resulted in countless millions of people entering the Kingdom of God and influenced and changed every strata of human life and institution. "Judge for your-selves whether it is right in God's sight to obey you," they declared to the Sanhedrin – a religious body granted power by the Roman rulers – "for we cannot help speaking what we have seen and heard."

Such a stand is being taken by Christians today in Nepal, the Hindu kingdom in the Himalayas. Christians there are frequently beaten up, arrested and jailed for their witness, one of the latest being a 75-year-old pastor. Yet the Church has multiplied in the face of persecution.

And despite their suffering, Christians – as Charles Mendies emphasised – are unstintingly loyal to their coun-try and King Birenda. But while seeking to be model citi-zens, they are obeying the higher call to preach the Gospel despite the consequences of their disobedience to the State which, in Charles' case, resulted in him being jailed for six years recently. That's true patriotism.

 **Oh, Lord, may I never shrink from spreading the Good News of your Kingdom.**

**Q** *Why not pray right now for Charles Mendies and the suffering Church in Nepal?*

*Have you found yourself in an Acts 4:19,20 situation?*

**DAY 7**

**Matthew 5:13–16; Esther 4:12–16; Daniel 5:1–17**

The 20th century is the pathetic story of trying to live by the bread of political power alone, according to Paul Johnson. That's why it's vital that Christians don't abandon the political arena even though "progress there is elusive, excruciatingly slow or non-existent", as Charles Colson put it in his uncomfortably fascinating book, *Against the Night*. "We must dig in for the long haul."

It was certainly a long haul for William Wilberforce. It took 38 years of campaigning inside and outside Parliament before he succeeded in getting slavery totally abolished. As I write, the opening shots of a new round in the 20-year battle to reduce the number of late abortions has just begun, with Christian MPs to the fore. "If we don't succeed now, we'll be back again," declared Anne Widdecombe. This Christian tenacity is the kind of salt in society Jesus was talking about.

Lack of salt has had a disastrous effect on society. William Carey, the 19th century shoemaker missionary to India, battled for 25 years to have *sati*, the burning of widows on their husbands' funeral pyres, abolished. Today, with Christian influence on the decline, *sati* is on the rise again, pointed out Vishal Mangalwadi, an evangelist and socio-political activist.

So many of today's politicians make a grave mistake similar to that of king Belshazzar, who trampled on the faith and secularised until there was no place for God. Daniel's counsel was ignored until disaster struck. Today's political decision-making promotes the idols of our time, especially the cult of self – unrestrained rights to happiness, power and sex instead of God's values such as fidelity in marriage, righteousness, justice and honesty in business. It is for the Church of Jesus Christ to stand on God's Word against these idols, for once it allows itself to be shaped by them it is doomed to failure.

Lord, may your standards be a strong influence in today's political decision-making. Give courage to those called to battle for you in the State corridors of power.

---

## FOR GROUP DISCUSSION

● Genesis 9:5,6 shows that God introduced the death penalty for murder. In the light of this and the apostle Paul's statement in Romans 13:4 about the ruler bearing the sword as punishment, discuss whether or not the return of capital punishment would be right for your country.

● What forms of protest against injustice would you consider right for Christians to make?

● What tensions do you experience between giving to Caesar what is Caesar's and giving to God what is God's?

● If you had a free choice in being able to introduce a piece of urgently needed legislation, what would it be?

● CARE (Christian Action, Research and Education) has 300 action groups in the UK as part of its ministry to influence the political sphere. What do you think about either forming such a group or joining an existing one? (Details from: CARE, 53 Romney Street, London SW1P 3RF).

● In seeking to use your vote wisely, what factors would influence who you vote for in a General or local election?

● Does it matter which party a Christian MP belongs to?

---

### Suggested further reading

*Kingdoms in Conflict* Charles Colson (Hodder & Stoughton)
*Against the Night* Charles Colson (Hodder & Stoughton)
*Render Unto Caesar* Herbert Carson (Monarch)
*Truth and Social Reform* Vishal Mangalwadi (Hodder & Stoughton)
*Wilberforce* John Pollock (Lion)
*Shaftesbury* John Pollock (Hodder & Stoughton)
*Poor is No Excuse* Jun Vencer (Paternoster).

# PEACE ON EARTH?

## Eddit Tait

**DAY 1**    **Ecclesiastes 3:1–8; John 16:33; Ephesians 2:13–18**

Peace. It's the one thing that people want most. Mankind longs for a world totally free of war, pain, suffering, death and destruction. Some people fight for peace, others protest and demonstrate for it, governments talk with other governments about it. Still others pray for it, Christians included.

Presidents George Bush and Mikhail Gorbachev finished their Malta summit with the announcement of a "new era of peace", while the international Press hailed "an end to the Cold War" which has existed at various low temperatures between East and West for over 40 years. Could it be true, especially in the wake of the tremendous changes which have been taking place on the Eastern European political map? Yet the fact remains that the world is more violent than it has ever been. The 20th century has seen more wars than in any other, while terrorism has increased year by year.

The Bible says that wars are a feature of this present age – "a time for war and a time for peace" – with Jesus, the "Prince of Peace" (Isa. 9:7), prophesying that wars and rumours of war would actually *increase* as the time draws near for His return to this earth (Matt. 24:6).

But there is a peace available to us now, the most important peace of all – peace of heart and mind through repentance of sins and having a personal relationship with God through Christ's sacrifice for us on the Cross. That kind of peace means that no matter what happens to our nation or the nations around us, we can rest in the fact that God is in control of the present and the future, as He has been in the past (Ps. 46:1–11). Yet it's not a selfish peace, for Jesus said,

"Blessed are the peacemakers" (Matt. 5:9). Those of us who are at peace with Him should be peacemakers by sharing His peace with others.

 **Lord, thank you that you have promised peace of heart and mind even though wars rage on this earth and will do so until the end of this present age.**

 *Are you at peace? If not, talk it over with the Prince of Peace.*

*How are you doing as a peacemaker?*

# DAY 2

**Jeremiah 17:9; Psalm 14:1–3; Romans 3:10–18, 23; 5:12; 13:4**

War is utterly terrible. The glorification of war is totally unacceptable for the Christian. Yet there are times when it is totally necessary, when the alternative is rampant, unrestrained wickedness. God is both the God of love (1 John 4:8) and the God of war (Ex. 15:3; Ps. 144:1) because He sees the wickedness in men's hearts. People want peace but want nothing to do with the God of peace, which is why there can be no complete worldwide peace.

Despite all the peace efforts down the centuries, God's word remains: "There is no peace for the wicked" (Isa. 48:22; 1 Thess. 5:3). Man's evil is the root cause of war. Adam's sin (Gen. 3:1–24) affected the whole human race. It was man's evil which caused him to invent weapons of war. So all of God's dealings with men and women since Adam have been with a fallen race in a corrupted environment. He instituted government, as we have seen in the previous section, to restrain evil – and that includes the use of force, to "bear the sword" (Rom. 13:4).

The sword of the State is wielded for the protection of citizens from rebellion within the country and also from the threat of evil from outside, when a country is in danger of losing its freedom and national entity through invasion from other, territory-hungry nations. Maintaining internal law and order is the job of police, magistrates and judges, with the latter given the power to impose the death penalty for murder (Gen. 9:6). Protection against evil from outside is the task of the armed forces.

Lord God, thank you that my country's armed forces are for the protection of the citizens, including myself. May the forces always be used only for the role which you have ordained.

 *Does today's study affect your view of the cause of war?*

*Have you reasons to thank God for your country's armed forces?*

 **Hebrews 11:32–34; Genesis 14:5–20; Nehemiah 4:6–23**

The proper use of armed forces is supported throughout the Bible, even though that meant annihilation at times, right down to the last man, woman and child (Josh. 10:28-42). God used the army to destroy the idolatry in the surrounding nations. The Lord took such drastic steps to preserve a people among Israel who weren't polluted by heathen practices. Such incidents form the bulk of the books of Deuteronomy, Joshua and Judges. Not a word is said against the leaders and, as we see by our first passage, Gideon, Barak, Samson and Jepthah are included in the roll call of the saints.

They were commended for their faith and obedience in responding to the call of the hour to set Israel free from the oppressing heathen nations – and lead their nation back to God's ways. Their names were next to David, the warrior king who did more than anyone to defeat Israel's heathen enemies. God had allowed other nations to invade and enslave Israel because the people had turned their backs on God. But when Israel repented, it was the turn of occupying nations to be judged for their wickedness. Later on, God's answer to Habakkuk's prayer was to send in the brutal, merciless Chaldeans as judgment on Israel (Hab.1:1–12ff). They, in turn, were overthrown by the Medes and Persians.

The first recorded instance of the raising and use of a national army was when Abraham responded to the invasion by Kedorlaomer and his cronies. His small, but trained band of 318 men gained total success by defeating the enemy and rescuing cousin Lot and his companions unharmed. Courageous and professional though they were, the real reason for their success was because "God Most High ... delivered your enemies into your hand."

Nehemiah's experience in arming his people against attack while restoration of the Jerusalem city wall went on illustrates both the need to defend freedom and the deterrent effect of weaponry in a fallen world. While there is – rightly – great alarm over the stockpiling of nuclear weapons and we Christians should support and pray for multilateral abandonment of them, the fact is that fear of their awesome power has prevented a global war for 40 years. That bears out the statement that restraint is ensured by "a strong man, fully armed" (Luke 11:21). No defence is no defence against attack when we realise the evil that lies in men's hearts.

 **Lord, thank you that you know man's heart through and through – and you have ordained safeguards so that evil does not triumph over good.**

 *Spend at least a bit of time praying for all nations to give up their reliance upon nuclear weapons.*

*Is there an alternative to the nuclear deterrent in this fallen, corrupt world?*

 **Luke 3:7–14; Matthew 8:5–10; Acts 10:1–7; 24–47**

John the Baptist was an earthy sort of fellow. When he preached, he always flew like an arrow to the point. "Repent!" was his cry. And calling the crowd a "brood of vipers" wasn't exactly the best way to win friends. Then some soldiers came up to him in response to his appeal for people to turn from their wicked ways. You might have thought that they would get the book thrown at them when they asked what they should do next. Like quit the army, for a start.

But no. John told them to be a credit to their profession, which meant no more threatening a spear through the throat if their victim didn't hand over his cash or drumming up false charges for an innocent person. "Live within your means" was John's parting exhortation. There was nothing wrong with soldiery, but the abuses associated with the profession were.

Neither did Jesus himself condemn the armed forces. In fact, his highest words of commendation were reserved for the Roman centurion who recognised, as few around him recognised, that Jesus was the Son of God who could heal His sick daughter with a word there and then. Later, the centurion in charge of the execution party at the Cross recognised Jesus for who He is and worshipped God. Then there was Centurion Cornelius, a man instrumental in opening the door for the Gospel to the Gentiles. None of those soldiers were counselled to pack their bags and go back to Rome, which all goes to show that one can be a committed Christian *and* serve in the armed forces.

The apostle Paul was grateful to Roman soldiers, too. They saved him from the lynch mob (Acts 21:30-36) and later provided an armed escort on a night journey to Caesarea to thwart a plot to kill him (Acts 23:12-33). The legitimate forces had upheld the law, protected a citizen's life and triumphed over anarchy.

 Lord, thank you for the examples of the Roman soldiers who became soldiers of Christ. Help me to be one whom you can commend for faith and service to you.

 *Bearing in mind what John the Baptist said to the soldiers, what would you say to members of an occupying power's armed forces?*

*What particular pressures and opportunities do Christian Servicemen and women face that you could pray about? Pray, too, for the work of the Officers' Christian Union and SASRA (Soldiers' and Airmen's Scripture Readers' Association).*

 **DAY 5**

**Deuteronomy 20:10–12; 2 Timothy 2:3 & 4; Exodus 20:13**

Having trained armed forces is one thing, but using them is another. Going to war should, in fact, be a last resort. Every effort to gain the required result without resorting to bloodshed must be taken. Only if the opposing side refuses to back down can force morally be used.

War can only be justified if evil really has been done –

where, for example, a country takes over another country against the people's wishes and enslaves them. Another criteria is whether the motive is just or whether the government seeks to gain more territory for itself. Objectives must be limited, the conflict finished as quickly as possible, every precaution taken to keep civilian casualties to the minimum and only as much force as necessary used. And while God tolerates war, He also imposes restraints, such as proper treatment of prisoners-of-war – and He abhors atrocities (2 Chron. 28:9). Yet even with trying to ensure that these safeguards are adhered to, war is never neat and tidy – and atrocities do take place and civilians suffer terribly.

Such considerations will particularly exercise Christians serving in the armed forces, along with being free of hatred for their enemies or acting out of vengeance. Charles Bester refused to serve in the South African army because it would have meant, as a white man, being willing to take violent action even to the point of killing black fellow countrymen in maintaining the government's apartheid stand. He was given a six-year prison sentence.

Christians are, of course, divided over the whole question of going to war at all and, more particularly, over whether a Christian should take up the profession of arms. Many would point to Exodus 20:13 as God's command not to kill. Modern Bible translations such as the New International Version translate *kill* as *murder,* a crime which, we have already seen, is punishable by death. The decision about whether to take up arms or not must, in the end, be made according to the individual's conscience (1 Cor. 10:29). One thing *is* certain, however – the presence of Christian officers, NCOs and other ranks has greatly influenced the moral quality of the armed forces down the years, as well as drawing colleagues to the Lord Jesus Christ.

 Lord, may justice be done among the nations and may war only be used as a last resort to deal with evil.

 *What criterion do you think justifies a nation going to war?*

*What are the objections against ever going to war and what do you think about them?*

**DAY 6**

Matthew 24:1–14; 1 Thessalonians 5:1–11; John 14:27

Wars have dominated the 20th century. There were 207 of them between 1900 and 1985, claiming 78 million military and civilian lives. Both the frequency and magnitude of the carnage have increased since the end of World War II. No other century has witnessed warfare on this scale. Worldwide military spending in 1988 was over one trillion dollars (approximately £641,025,641,025), six per cent of the total gross national product. International military spending exceeds that which goes on education, health and foreign aid.

It is all evidence that we are living in the last days of this present age, for Jesus prophesied that war and rumours of wars would increase as the end drew near – together with an escalation of famines and earthquakes, which have also been a feature of the past few years.

Our Lord foretold that warfare and suffering would characterise the years until His second coming. At the time He said this, the world was enjoying great peace and stability under the Romans. The empire was expanding and trouble spots were being dealt with and brought under effective rule. Under the *Pax Romana* (Roman peace) it was possible to travel and go about one's daily business throughout the Mediterranean lands without fear of attack. It was a kind of golden era. So Jesus might have been taken for a prophet of gloom and doom.

Yet 40 years after His statement, the Roman army invaded Israel and wreaked destruction and carnage. Some four hundred years later the Roman empire was itself destroyed by the barbarians, with even greater loss of life. And wars have been the pattern of earthly life since, especially this century. Jesus was a realist rather than a pessimist, for as He looked down the centuries through prophetic eyes – and into the evil hearts of men – He knew that no pact between nations can bring about lasting peace.

 Lord, thank you that your Word is true and what you have said will happen, both to this earth and in the hearts of mankind.

 *At what point should a country limit its defence build-up?*

*How many deaths could be avoided in Ethiopia and other places where localised conflicts are going on if the worldwide arms trade was halted?*

**DAY 7**

**Isaiah 2:4; Revelation 11:15;19:11–21**

The United Nations headquarters in New York has a motto on one of its walls — today's first Scripture, which so optimistically proclaims that nations "will beat their swords into ploughshares and their spears into pruning hooks. Nation will not take up sword against nation, neither shall they learn war any more." It's easy to see why the UN chose that verse: worldwide peace, what a prospect! But just as Jesus was realistic, so should we be. That Scripture refers to the end of the age, after the final great battle in which Jesus, the warrior King of kings, will overthrow Satan and all the earth's rulers who are opposed to Him. Then He will reign over the whole earth and there will be that longed-for peace.

In the meantime, we Christians are called to be faithful in this fallen, imperfect world, and to work within the structures God has instituted for a measure of law and order. That *may* mean serving in the armed forces — it certainly means being committed to being peacemakers wherever we can. The most effective way of being peacemakers is to proclaim the Gospel, which is the most powerful antidote of war. An increasing number of ex-terrorists in places like Northern Ireland can testify to that fact, having found that Christ's peace is the greatest discovery of all.

Nor, of course, must we neglect prayer, especially for governments in their search for peace (1 Tim. 2:1,2). Battling in prayer is something all Christians are called to do, whatever our views about going to war and serving in the armed forces may be. We must wage war in the heavenlies against Satan's forces in Christ's name (2 Cor. 10:4-6; Eph. 6:10-18) until the day dawns when the imperfect gives way to the perfect reign of Christ and complete peace becomes a wonderful reality.

Lord Jesus, thank you that you are coming back to this earth to reign and usher in perfect peace. Help me, in the meantime, to be both a peacemaker and an effective Christian soldier – whether I am a member of my country's armed forces or not.

## FOR GROUP DISCUSSION

• How much peace do you think can be achieved during this present age?

• It's a fallacy to believe that we can achieve national and international peace when individuals are at war with one another, Christians being guilty of this as well (Jas.4:1–3). Discuss this problem.

• The struggle of a country to gain independence is a frequent cause of war. How much are colonial powers at fault through hanging on to territory they have gained?

• In the light of our study on Day 5, was Britain's decision to go to war over the Falklands justified?

• Do you think being a Christian and serving in the armed forces are compatible?

• "The calculation that we should be safe by leaving the Bomb only in the hands of our adversaries is one that no responsible public man with any insight into human nature would ever make." Discuss this statement by Cambridge Dean Dr Edward Norman.

• Can you think of any country which has unilaterally laid down its armaments and surrounding nations have followed suit?

• Do you think bombing a city flat is justified in war or should raids be restricted to military targets only?

### Suggested further reading

*Peace in Our Time?* David Atkinson (Inter-Varsity Press)
*Render Unto Caesar* (chapter 10) Herbert Carson (Monarch)
*Target Earth* General Editor: Frank Kaleb Jansen (University of the Nations/Global Mapping International)
*The Man of Lawlessness* Tom Davies (Hodder & Stoughton).

# WHO IS MY NEIGHBOUR?

## Patrick Sookhdeo

*Patrick Sookhdeo comes from Guyana and is Director of In Contact Ministries based at the St Andrew's Centre, Plaistow, in London's East End. Married to Rosemary, a New Zealander, he was an Evangelical Alliance staff member before founding In Contact to help churches understand immigrants and ethnic minorities and reach them for Christ. Courses are run at the centre to equip Christians for working among ethnic people in Britain and among other cultures overseas. Racially integrated churches have been planted. Various types of practical caring ministries go hand in hand with evangelism.*

**DAY 1**

**Genesis 1:26–31**

*God moulded man out of clay and put him in the oven to bake. But when God opened the oven to take out the man, He found He had baked him too long, for the man was black. So He made another man and baked him just a short while. But when God took this man out of the oven he was still white. So God made yet another man and this time He baked him for just the right time, for he came out of the oven a beautiful brown, just like the Indian.*

So runs a Hindu story of creation. From the first chapter of the Bible, however, we learn that God did not make three types of human being, but one, whom He commanded to increase and fill the earth. So from one man "he made every nation of men, that they should inhabit the whole earth" (Acts 17:26). The entire population of the world is one family. We do not read in verse 27 of today's passage "black and white he created them." The only difference is male and female. So there is one human race, with Adam and Eve our first parents.

Man has been created in the image or likeness of God. "In his image" it emphasises, in case we have missed the point. So every member of the human family is made in the image of God. It is so easy to slip into thinking that I am the norm or standard and – as in the Hindu creation story – those who differ are sub-standard. All people have equal worth and dignity, all are equally valued by Him. Everyone is special!

 **Lord, thank you that you have made all peoples of the world. Help me today to see your image in everyone I meet.**

 *In what ways have you been enriched by meeting people of other races and cultures? Food, fashion, music, or anything else?*

*Honestly identify your own prejudices based on skin colour and ask God to help you deal with them.*

 **Exodus 23:9; Leviticus 19:33,34; Deuteronomy 10:18,19; 24:17–22**

God's command to Adam and Eve was to multiply and fill the earth. Here is the recognition that the earth belongs to God, not to any single group. And we are stewards of earth – not owners. In the first five books of the Bible there are frequent references to the alien, stranger, foreigner and sojourner – the immigrant. All this speaks of God's love and concern for such people and His desire that they should be treated correctly.

This theme is picked up again by some of the prophets, who condemn those who ill-treat or oppress the alien (Ezek. 22:29; Mal. 3:5). Nationalism is a sin. Discrimination in any form is an offence not just against mankind, but also against God himself.

Aliens, along with other vulnerable groups such as the fatherless and widows, are especially loved by God (Deut. 10:18). We, too, are to love the alien. "Love him as yourself" (Lev. 19:33) and "have the same law for the alien and the native-born" (Lev. 24:22; Num. 15:14–16).

We can follow God's own example and show our love by providing practical assistance to those in need (Deut. 10:18) or, as Jesus teaches in the parable of the sheep and the goats, we can invite strangers into our homes (Matt. 25:34–40). One way that Israelite farmers could show practical loving care for the alien was not to harvest their crops too greedily, but leave some to be gleaned (Deut. 24:19–21). This reminds us of Ruth and how she, a Moabitess, gleaned in the fields of Boaz, an Israelite, married him and became the great grandmother of King David – and part of Jesus' human ancestry.

 **Lord, thank you that you welcome us into your family as you welcomed Ruth. Help me to welcome others into my country – and my home and church.**

 *In Deuteronomy 1:16, God commands that there should be no partiality when judging between native-born and alien. Is this command obeyed in Britain today?*

*"Your people will be my people and your God my God," said Ruth to Naomi (Ruth 1:16). You may be happy to share your Saviour with others, but are you willing to share yourself?*

## DAY 3

**Philippians 3:20; 1 Peter 2:9–12**

The Early Church father, Tertullian, described Christians as "the third race" – neither Jew nor Gentile, neither slave nor free, neither cultured nor uncultured, but God's new community. Yesterday we studied God's command to love the alien. He gave it because the Israelites themselves had been aliens when they were slaves in Egypt – they knew what it felt like to live in a foreign land. But how can we Christians apply this to ourselves?

Peter gives us the answer. We are aliens, too – strangers, exiles, foreigners. The Greek words he uses describe someone who is a resident in a country which is not his own – a temporary resident whose homeland is elsewhere, who is not a citizen in the place he happens to be because he belongs to another country.

When someone puts their faith in Jesus Christ, they are born again as a citizen of heaven, which means they are no longer a native-born citizen of the world. Being in the world but not of it is an uncomfortable situation and produces tensions, but it should make us specially able to understand what an immigrant feels like. We should be able to understand why they wonder, "Who am I? What is my identity?"

Who better to understand the immigrant than the Christian, an immigrant on planet Earth!

 **Lord, thank you for the new life you have given me and for my home in heaven. Help me to understand those who do not know where they belong.**

 *Do I feel ill at ease or comfortable in the world?*

*Which is the greater influence — me on the world or the world on me?*

**DAY 4**

**Matthew 2:13–15**

A man arrived in Britain some years ago as a refugee from the Middle East. Back home he had been brutally tortured for his political beliefs. He felt lost, alone, abused, unwanted and was suffering severe psychological stress. Then he was converted to Christ. Immediately he had peace, joy and a sense of belonging.

There are many such refugees here in Britain. They come from various parts of the world, seeking refuge from political oppression, economic exploitation or religious persecution. It is predicted that the number of refugees worldwide will rise dramatically over the next few years.

The Bible has frequent references about people who have to flee from trouble to safety. Our Lord Jesus had to – He, along with His parents, were refugees when He was very young. Threatened by king Herod, they fled to Egypt, a country known to give refuge from tyranny, persecution and other dangers. Jesus' earthly parents knew what it was to experience loneliness, hardship, persecution and rejection, as well as to be accepted in a foreign land, dependent on others' kindness and goodness.

May God help us always to have open hearts and arms for those in need and distress.

Heavenly Father, thank you that your Son, Jesus, under-stood what it means to be an outcast. Give wisdom to those in authority to act with justice and compassion — and show me what part I can play.

 *Try to imagine what it feels like to be a refugee in a strange land. How would you like to be treated?*

*If there are no refugees in your area, who is there who feels lonely, unaccepted and needs your love?*

**DAY 5**

**Luke 10:25–37**

"Neighbours, everybody needs good neighbours," goes the TV theme song. But who is my neighbour? A politician once gave his definition: "My neighbour is my family, close friends and those from my own culture, group and community." But Jesus' answer is vastly different, as the parable of the good Samaritan emphasises.

The Jew (we are specifically told he was in Jewish territory, too) was badly beaten, stripped and left half-dead on a road notorious for brigands. His fellow Jews flatly refused to come to his aid, but a despised foreigner rescued him. The Samaritan's tremendous compassion took him right across the cultural and religious barriers in an act which cost considerable time and money, as well as risking his own safety.

An elderly English lady lives alone in an inner city area. Her next-door neighbours are Pakistani Muslims. She can hardly get out and about so is often in need of basic food and other things. The Pakistani couple care for her as if she was their mother, frequently being seen taking food to her. This is a not uncommon situation. Like the Samaritan in Jesus' story, true love and compassion are shown by those who have been despised to those who had previously despised them.

We are responsible for all those around us. Anyone of any nation who is in need is our neighbour.

 Thank you, Lord, for all those who have helped me, often at great cost to themselves. Help me to be willing to be used by you to help others.

*Very likely the priest and the Levite felt sorry for the man lying on the road, but they did nothing to help him. In what practical ways can you show love and compassion to those around you?*

*How costly is it to be a good neighbour?*

**John 4:7–27; 1 John 4:7–18**

The world in which Jesus lived was full of barriers. We see him crossing several barriers in His dealings with the Samaritan woman. There was the racial barrier to get over – the woman came from a mixed ethnic background. **Religion was** another barrier – the Samaritan version was corrupted. She had a moral barrier, for she had had several husbands and was living in sin.

And there was the sex discrimination barrier, for in that society men had no dealings with women. As a Jewish prayer goes: "Lord God of heaven, I thank Thee Thou hast not made me a slave – blessed be Thy Name. Lord God of Heaven I thank Thee Thou hast not made me a woman – blessed be Thy Name."

Jesus calls us to be barrier-crossers, not to be self-righteous. We are to love and accept people, whoever they are and whatever their background – not to reject and despise them.

Because God is love, we ought to love each other. If we do this, God dwells in us and His love is perfected in us. Fear will be well and truly dealt with. It is often fear that turns differences into barriers. We fear the unfamiliar and unknown or being misunderstood, doing the wrong thing or being shown up as we encounter the other person. Yet if we allow God's love to really dwell in us we will never be afraid, but live in openness and acceptance of others.

**Fill me so full with your love, Lord, that there is no room for fear, and show me how to use the opportunities you give me to tell others about you.**

*What differences have you allowed to become barriers?*
*How much does fear hinder you from sharing the Gospel?*

**Galatians 3:26–28; Revelation 7:9–12**

Newly-arrived in Britain one winter in the 1950s, a West Indian went to a church some distance from where he was living and joined in the worship. The following Sunday he went back to that church – but was not allowed in. That incident led to the formation of one of the largest black-led denominations in Britain.

There were men and women from many different backgrounds and cultures in the Early Church. The leadership of the Church at Antioch was both multiracial and multi-cultural (Acts 13:1). Christ broke down the dividing wall of hostility so that all believers are one in Him (Eph. 2:14). When discrimination did surface in the Early Church – the treatment of the Greek-speaking widows (Acts 6:1–6) and Peter and others' refusal to eat with Gentiles (Gal. 2:11–13) for example – steps were taken to put things right.

Sadly, Christians in Britain are divided – not just by denominations, but by race and culture. Many black Christians feel unwanted and have often experienced prejudice and discrimination in churches. We must affirm that we are all one in Jesus (Gal. 3:28), for the fact is that we all share the same Holy Spirit (Phil. 2:1) and are all inheritors of the same Kingdom.

 Lord, thank you for the rich diversity within your Church. Help me always to appreciate this.

---

### FOR GROUP DISCUSSION

● If a Hindu or Muslim family moved in next door to you, what would you do?

● What would be your attitude if your children became very friendly with ethnic children at school?

● How much do we pigeon-hole and treat people according to their appearance? (See James 2:1–4.) Why do you think race is a barrier?

● It is said that 11 o'clock on a Sunday morning in the USA is the most segregated hour of the week. What is your church doing about this problem?

● Do you consider people from other cultures to be harder to reach for Christ than English people?

# EVERY TRIBE AND NATION

## Patrick Johnstone

*Patrick Johnstone is Director of Research at WEC International at Bulstrode, Gerrards Cross. He is author of* Operation World *(STL/ WEC), an indispensable prayer atlas which is packed with information for prayer about every country of the world. With his wife, Jill, he first began gathering world prayer needs as a missionary in southern Africa and continues to travel widely, motivating young people in particular to commit themselves to mission as well as being involved in strategic planning.*

**Genesis 11:1–9; 12:1–3**

The tower of Babel is the extraordinary account of the confusion of languages and the start of the peoples of the world. There are over 7,000 known languages, so God certainly did an effective job of confusing them!

From that episode onwards, the Scriptures show how God reaches out to the peoples of the world to redeem them from the sin that made the confusion necessary. So it is hardly surprising that the judgment of Genesis 11 is followed by God making a covenant to bless the nations through Abraham (Gen. 12:3).

God called Abraham for one supreme purpose – a purpose far, far greater than blessing him, his family or even the nations that would physically be his descendants. *All* the families (peoples) of the earth would be blessed and become his spiritual descendants. The promise of Genesis 12:3 is referred to again and again in both the Old and New Testaments. As the apostle Paul says "...and the scripture, foreseeing that God would justify the Gentiles by faith, preached the Gospel beforehand to Abraham, saying 'in you shall all the nations be blessed'" (Gal. 3:8 RSV; also see vv. 6,7 & 9).

Our God is a missionary God, seeking out those of every

nation and people who will be sons of Abraham by faith. His great concern for every people is revealed more clearly in the New Testament. Isn't it wonderful that, right at the birth of the Church, men and women heard the mighty works of God in their own language! The sin and confusion of Babel has been dealt with through the Cross and by Pentecost.

 **Lord, give me a missionary heart like yours, with a deep concern for the scattered and unreached peoples of the world. May other nations be blessed through me!**

 *Does the theory of evolution offer any logical alternative to this account of the origin of languages? The Creation Resources Trust (Mead Farm, Downhead, West Camel, Yeovil, Somerset, BA22 7RQ) may be of help to you.*

*How many of the world's 7,000 languages have (a) a Bible, (b) a New Testament, (c) a Scripture portion, (d) a Gospel recording, (e) a translation team? How many translators are still needed? (Check the publications of the Bible Society and Wycliffe Bible Translators or refer to my book Operation World).*

## DAY 2

### Psalm 22:1–31

The power and pathos of this psalm is awesome. The suffering Saviour is prophetically revealed. Yet the vision of the forsaken, battered, torn, pierced figure of He who died for me tends to anaesthetise my mind from seeing the glorious triumph at the end of the passage. Jesus died (vv.1–21), rose again (vv. 22–26) and was raised to His glorious throne, from where He now reigns (vv. 27–31).

These final five verses reveal the purpose of His suffering and resurrection – that all ends of the earth might turn to the Lord and that all the families of the nations should worship Him. Here, again, is an echo of the promise given to Abraham (Gen. 12:3). At the heart of the work of the Cross is world evangelisation. Any Christian organisation or activity that does not unite these two is unscriptural! Yet for centuries the Church has divorced them.

We are told in verse 30 of a posterity that will serve Him and, by implication, see a future generation fully evangelised. We are that posterity! We could be that final generation who will see the Gospel spread to every country and every people in the world.

Jesus reigns today (v. 28) amidst the upheavals and turmoil taking place on our planet. All will, sooner or later, bow the knee. We can expect victory because He *is* victorious. Let's expect a completion of world evangelisation!

 **Lord, I want to be part of that posterity that serves you. I don't want to be left out of what you are doing in the world today. I am willing to do anything you ask and go wherever you lead, so that men and women of peoples yet unreached may hear the Good News and respond in repentance to you.**

 *Where in the psalm is the promise that every single people group will worship God? (Also see Rev. 7:9; Matt. 24:14).*

*Look up Old Testament references to "the ends of the earth," and "all peoples".*

 **Matthew 28:16–20; Mark 16:14–20**

Have you ever noticed how one theme dominates Jesus' post-resurrection ministry? The end of the gospels of Matthew, Mark and Luke and the beginning of Acts all record the charge and the challenge our Lord gave to His disciples: to evangelise the world. We call it either the Great Commission or the Great Sending Out. Christ's concern was that the disciples, followed by the Church throughout the ages, should place world evangelisation at the top of the agenda. Yet for many in the Church, the Great Commission has become the *great omission*!

Yet look at what Jesus commands us to do! We must go to all nations to make disciples. The Greek word actually means *peoples* – an *ethnical*, not a *political* concept. All of us are commanded to go, the only question being "Where?" The obvious implication is that if we can find any evidence of the existence of people where there are no known

55

disciples, it is our business to change that.

There are probably about 12,000 people groups in the 222 nations and territories of the world. Of these, about 3,000 have no known groups of committed believers, and of these 1,000 have no one to even tell them how to become a disciple of Jesus Christ. An army of goers is still needed to finish the job!

 **Lord, I praise you that you have _all_ authority, so I don't need to fear your command to go. I want to be always in the centre of your will for my life so that you can use me to the full.**

 *What are the differences in the Great Commission recorded in Matthew and Mark?*

*What are the best ways to accomplish each command?*

**Acts 1:1–11**

"Famous last words" is a popular expression. But surely the most important famous last words were uttered by the most famous of all persons who lived on earth. "You shall be my witnesses," said Jesus just before He returned to heaven.

It is a command, a statement and a promise. Our Lord spoke of four specific areas where we should witness: Jerusalem, all Judea, Samaria and to the ends of the earth. The "and" is important – every Christian has a responsibility for all four areas, for the whole world. God makes no distinction between local evangelism and foreign missions. Christians should be equally concerned about them, for we abuse the Scriptures by separating them.

The Great Commission means you are a witness to:

1. Jerusalem – the place where you live.
2. Judea – the nation of which you are a part.
3. Samaria – the areas in your own land where strangers, immigrants, foreigners live. Many in our own country are like Samaritans: despised, avoided, feared. Yet so many are totally unreached with the Gospel.

4. The ends of the earth – whole areas such as the Middle East, southern Europe, the African Sahel, north India, central Asia, which are populated by hundreds of language groups and cultures who have never heard of the saving grace and power of Jesus.

Who am I, little me, to do anything about this unmet need? Praise God, the Holy Spirit has been given to empower us to speak of the Saviour of the world! So trust Him – you have nothing to fear.

 **Lord, make me your mouthpiece today! Lead me to someone, even of another race, with whom I can share about you.**

 *How can you equip yourself to tell your friends, relatives, neighbours and the people you meet each day about Jesus?*

*Ask the Lord to show you someone who needs praying through to salvation.*

**DAY 5**

**Romans 15:7–29**

Paul had a vision. He shared it with the Roman Christians he had never met. It was for the Gentiles to be reached with the Gospel. In this passage he quotes a lot from the Old Testament to prove God's concern for the Gentiles. He needed to, because the Christians from a Jewish background found that vision hard to accept. How similar today! So few Christians have any real concern for those who have never been reached with the Gospel, let alone for any outside their local area.

Paul had already achieved much. He had proclaimed the Gospel from Jerusalem to Illyricum (the whole of the north-east Mediterranean region). It is sobering to realise that this area, which includes Turkey, Greece, Albania and Yugoslavia, contains some of the most unreached peoples on earth today.

Yet the apostle wasn't satisfied with all that. The divine compulsion was on him to go beyond where the name of Jesus was known. He knew Spain had not been reached for the Master. There are those of this generation with such a passion. Are you one of them?

**Lord, give me a heart like Paul's, a vision of the unreached and of what I can do through you to get the Gospel to them.**

 *Write to a mission asking for a list of the unreached peoples to whom they have a desire to reach for Christ in the next five years.*

*Choose one unreached people and pray for that tribe every week until the Church is established among them.*

### Revelation 5:1–10; 8:1–5

This marvellous passage looks at the world from a heavenly perspective. We see the Lion of the tribe of Judah, the victorious Lamb who alone was worthy to open the seals of history. The Lord Jesus Christ is in total control of history, the nations, the myriad great events good and bad – and in total control of all that happens to you and me!

Yet in chapters 5 and 8 there is a remarkable reference to prayer. We, the redeemed, are a kingdom of priests to God – standing between a holy God and sinful man. Our prayers rise purified to the throne of the Lamb and bring fire on the earth. Prayer is the only earthly activity that is noticed in heaven. Prayer is vital to God's programme – hence the centre-point of the seventh seal.

Why all this prayer? The answer is revealed in the new song of heaven to the Lamb, who has been slain to ransom people from every tribe, language, people and nation (5:9). It is the prayers of the saints who are helping to bring the ransomed people in.

*Intercession* is an old-fashioned word which is regarded as outdated by many Christians in this press-the-button-and-out-comes-the-answer society. Yet intercessory prayer, especially pleading for God to pour out His Spirit upon this needy world and for people to hear and respond to His crucified, risen, ascended and glorified Son, is a vital part of evangelising the world.

 **Lord, put fire in my prayers so that they reach your throne and that, through them, the fires of revival and even judgment may be poured out upon earth.**

*Is there anything to stop your prayers getting answered? Meditate on 1 John 1:9 and James 5:16 – and ensure that your prayer line is kept clean.*

*Use such publications as* Operation World, Global Prayer Digest *and* Revival *magazine to guide you in praying for the peoples of the world.*

**Revelation 7:1–17**

During the chaotic end to our sin-sick world, another world is in preparation. A wonderful place where sorrow, tears, hunger and pain will be no more and where we will dwell in the presence of the Lamb. The redeemed will be there – from both Israel and the Gentiles. There will be a numberless throng of people from every race, tribe, people and tongue. It will be the fulfilment of God's plan – a bride for the Lamb to be with Him for evermore.

The effects of sin and the confusion of Babel are not only reversed, but the resulting variety which makes up the Body of Christ is more beautiful because of the Son of God's redemption on the Cross at Calvary.

There are hundreds of peoples in the world who are not yet adequately represented in the Body. What about the Pathans of Pakistan, the Tibetans of China, the Maures of Mauritania, the Macedonians of Yugoslavia, the Arabs of Qatar, the Turkmen of the USSR...? Who will tell them and disciple the converts, that they may take their place around the throne, too?

 **Lord Jesus, lead me to play my part in completing the evangelisation of the world, so that you may return soon because the job is done!**

## FOR GROUP DISCUSSION

• Why has this main theme of Scripture, the evangelisation of the world, usually been relegated to being a side issue in churches? What ought to be done about it?

• What is your involvement individually and corporately as a fellowship in promoting the speediest possible evangelisation of the world? What practical steps can be taken to improve this?

• Prayer is absolutely fundamental to any ministry, including missions. How seriously do you pray individually, as a family and as a church?

• What do you think about setting real targets for reaching the unreached? Like concentrating, as a house group or prayer group, on one specific people in prayer and actually taking the Gospel to them?

# SECTION 2
## THE FAMILY

# BATTLING FOR THE FAMILY

## Rob & Marion White

*Rob White is National Director of British Youth for Christ, based at Cleobury Place near Kidderminster, a 26-acre site developed as an evangelistic and training centre for young people. BYFC works alongside local churches in reaching young people in schools and on the streets. Marion, a trained teacher, is actively involved with Rob both in the ministry of BYFC and with Spring Harvest. The couple have three daughters, Jo, Debbie and Naomi, and have written a book on family life called* My Family, My Church *(published by Kingsway).*

**DAY 1**

### Ephesians 4:29 – 5:1–4

Words! Where would we be without them? Sometimes though, if you are anything like us, you probably wish that words had never been invented. Words can hurt, give and leave the wrong impression, and live on in the mind and heart of the receiver long after the one who spoke them has forgotten them. There is no more important place for the right exchange of words than in the family. Living with others means that, inevitably, words will often become hasty, cheap, sarcastic and wounding. While in other walks of life we would probably guard our words more carefully, we are prone to become careless with them in the family.

Surely, as we study these words from Ephesians, we are challenged about our use of words within the family. Christianity begins at home – and that means working on our communication. There must, of course, be time for communication. Maybe one of the reasons why our communication is poor is because we try to say important things in small spaces. We must make *quality* time for one another – parent/parent, parent/children.

Look again at Ephesians 4:29 – "Do not let any unwholesome talk come out of your mouths, but only what is helpful for building others up according to their needs..." Do you think before you speak? We parents need to be just as strict with ourselves as we are with our children. Badly chosen words delivered in anger can begin to destroy others, but carefully selected words will build up and encourage.

 **Forgive me, Lord Jesus, for the times I have wounded my marriage partner and my children with thoughtless words delivered in anger. Help me to choose my words so that they help rather than hurt.**

 *Is my family life important enough to me to give plenty of time for communication?*

*Review your use of words honestly. How many communicate anger, lack of real interest, genuine love, care and concern?*

 **Proverbs 22:6; Deuteronomy 6:1–9; 2 Timothy 1:1–5; 3:14–15**

We parents have a natural desire to teach our children to have a real interest in things we particularly enjoy and know something about. It might be football, cooking, knitting, music, train spotting, walking, mathematics...Yet how much more important it is to teach children about the Person who has transformed our lives! If God doesn't have first place in our lives and we put other things before Him, our children will soon see that the "spiritual" things we say to them are hypocrisy.

But if we have an earnest desire for them to learn about the One we love most, even though we make mistakes, they will accept that our faith is worth something and will be interested to know about it.

Commitment to bringing children up to know and love the Lord Jesus can begin even before they are born! Pray for your baby in the womb and when he or she is in the cot. Don't be embarrassed to pray in front of your children. Read them Bible stories, tell them about creation, the Cross and resurrection. There are many excellent children's books and tapes to help. Praise the Lord together (or if you're tone deaf just play the tapes!). Make the most of spontaneous moments to teach your youngsters about their

Saviour. Family worship times need to be exciting – we know of a family who made a den under their dining room table for this!

Don't leave it all to the Sunday school teachers. It is primarily our job, with Sunday school being a back-up. What a privilege it is to teach our children what we know of God – and a tremendous opportunity!

 **Help me, Lord, to teach my children what it really means to be a Christian – by my actions as well as my words.**

 *Think of ways in which you can improve your times of family worship and teaching.*

*Which aspect of your relationship with God would you like most of all to pass on to your children?*

 **Ephesians 6:1–4,10–18**

The battle is on! Family life is under fire. The pressures of society and its lack of moral values close in on the Christian family desperate to survive the pull of materialism, the strain of the mortgage, the temptations to flirt with the world. It might sound depressing but, in fact, it is a tremendous challenge to live a different lifestyle, to make our mark on society, to draw others to Jesus as they see that we have a strength beyond ourselves that enables us to swim against the tide.

So what's the answer to all this? Prayer, prayer and more prayer – family praying, husband and wife praying, individual praying, learning how to be aggressive against the enemy in a good dose of 100 per cent spiritual warfare.

Start with the apostle Paul's command: stand firm against the enemy. Don't be brow-beaten by Satan – he was well and truly defeated at Calvary! Husbands, take up the battle on behalf of your wives, for you know their weak areas. Wives, take a similar kind of stance for your husbands. Mums and Dads, your children need you to stand firm for them. Teach them how they can put on the armour and resist the enemy themselves. Even at five years old, school can be a real battlefield for your youngsters, so pray every morning before they leave home, pray for them while they are at school – and don't give up!

Our daughters are teenagers now and face many temptations, but we must not be tempted to despair or give up if the situation looks bleak. Remember, the outcome of the battle is already decided – and we are on the winning side!

 **Help me not to fear, Lord, when the enemy presses hard, but remember that the battle belongs to you and that you are the victor.**

 *When did you last spend time praying for your husband/wife?*

*Do you know what problems each of your children are struggling most with at the moment?*

 **Proverbs 13:24; Hebrews 12:5–13**

Does the Bible you're reading say *rod*? It's not exactly a word to fire us with enthusiasm about Scriptural teaching on discipline! Yet it bears a foundational truth about the proper upbringing of a child. Discipline has become a dirty word in some circles – even in some Christian circles! Freedom of expression seems to be encouraged not only in the media and arts, but also in school and home. But we're sure you parents know better, that you regard discipline as important. But can you discipline in a disciplined way?

Because discipline is very much part of God's relationship to us, His children, we must be serious about it with our children. We've got to think it through carefully.

The main issue is how much does proper discipline cost parents and how much does it cost the children. "It hurts me more than it hurts you" is a phrase that many of us heard when we were kids. Now we probably say it to *our* children! But whether we actually say it or not, we almost definitely think it. That's where proper discipline often goes wrong – it hurts parents too much. It hurts to see the children hurting, it hurts us because, in the midst of the pressures of daily life, we don't want any more hassles. It hurts because we would rather not have confrontation and because, being tired enough already, our energy is sapped even more through disciplining.

Yet if we don't grasp the issue of discipline fearlessly and carefully, we will end up seeing our children hurt far more and probably long-term, than they will ever be through the temporary hurt of disciplinary acts.

 **Father God, I see that I must not shirk my responsibilities to properly discipline the children you have given me. Help me to do so for their sakes and for the sake of your Kingdom.**

 *In what ways have you experienced God's discipline?*

*How much time do you and your marriage partner spend talking together and praying about disciplining your children?*

**DAY 5**

**Psalm 68:4–6; Luke 14:11–14**

God makes a home for the lonely! Have you stopped to think how that might be possible? It's true that God himself can comfort and bring companionship to a lonely life, but it's more likely that He wants to use us, His body here on earth, to make a home for the lonely. What a privilege to know that God wants to use our family life for the outworking of His purposes!

It's no excuse to say that we can't invite anyone into our home because we need a new carpet in the lounge and the kitchen needs redecorating. A lonely person only notices the warmth of friendship, the togetherness of the family and the sharing of our lives.

You don't have to be lavish entertainers – hospitality can simply be a cup of tea or coffee and a biscuit or a sandwich. There are so many lonely people who would just love to be invited into a home and be part of a real family, complete with all the noise, arguments, joys and sorrows of normal family life. When you share your home with others, it may well cost in time and privacy, but your whole family will be enriched by the lives of those who come through your front door.

Sometimes we need to be open to having an extended

family. If God is speaking to you about that, don't turn a deaf ear. Having someone living with us is not easy and we do need to count the cost. But rather than moan because it will unsettle your cosy existence, press forward and explore all the ways that God wants to use your family.

 **Dear Father, show us how our family and home can be used to glorify you.**

 *How many people have you given hospitality to recently?*

*Pinpoint someone — a neighbour, work colleague, school friend, who is lonely, pray for them and invite them into your home.*

**DAY 6**

**Luke 15:11–32**

It's not always easy to say sorry, is it? There's no difficulty when we've just trodden on someone's toe or spilt a mug of coffee on the lounge carpet, but it can be very difficult when we feel we are in the right, at least partially. There seems to be that something inside that squirms at the thought of apologising. The same with forgiveness. We may think that it is not too difficult to shoot out a quick "I forgive you" when another person has told us they are sorry, but truly forgiving someone who has offended, hurt or stung us in sensitive areas doesn't come naturally. Yet the well-known passage we are studying today shows just how important forgiveness in the family is — and just how damaging are resentment and bitterness when they grow in the soil of unforgiveness, as in the case of the prodigal's older brother.

This is, perhaps, more applicable when our children grow older. How hurt we feel about some of the things our offspring say or do! And how hurt our children can be at times by our short-tempered, ill-considered, boorish attitudes! Let forgiveness flow in your family — by asking for it and giving it. And that includes parents asking forgiveness from their children.

Forgiveness will really lay soothing ointment on our family relationships. We can make our mistakes, have our traumas and come through our battles if we are secure in the knowledge that we are good at forgiving each other.

Lack of forgiveness, on the other hand, is like a dam holding back the fresh flow of family love and harmony. It only leaves us with stale experiences and nostalgic memories.

 **Lord, help us never to allow resentment and bitterness to fester in the family, but to be quick to forgive and ask for forgiveness.**

 *Is there someone in your family against whom you are harbouring wrong feelings? If so, are you prepared to forgive them — unconditionally?*

*Think of all the qualities members of your family have — and thank God for them.*

### DAY 7

**Ephesians 4:31,32; Colossians 3:12–21**

So, now you've spent a week studying the Scriptures, read our notes about family life and acted on them where necessary, you have relationships par excellence! We doubt it — we haven't, even though we've written this section. It takes years to get right. By the time our children have flown the nest we may feel that we could bring up a family without so many mistakes. But by then, of course, there isn't the energy, inclination or even possibility of doing so!

Perseverance — that's the word! Prayerful perseverance and the determination to get it as right as we can. Today's verses are packed with good instruction, with Colossians 3:12–16 summing it all up most succinctly. The characteristics and attitudes outlined in these few verses can be the most immediately and beneficially expressed in family life.

Don't grow weary or lose heart. Seek advice where necessary. Don't forget that God really cares for the family — He is on your side and longing to help you. If one parent or one or more of the children seem to be drifting away from God, don't despair. You will obviously be full of concern and be very disappointed, but don't let the devil imprison you in discouragement.

Perhaps you could use this statement as a declaration for your family: "We purpose, by the strength and grace of God our heavenly Father, to stand strong against the wiles of the evil one in our family life. We purpose to maintain our unity, through adversity as well as the good times, praying together, loving and forgiving one another and building up one another with wholesome words of encouragement. We are determined to see our family used by God as a testimony to others around us, that we may see His Kingdom extended."

 **Heavenly Father, thank you that you love families and that my family is special to you. Help this family to be a living testimony to your love, grace and power, each member secure in a world that lacks security.**

---

### FOR GROUP DISCUSSION

- How much time should we spend with our children each day? Discuss how, in this hectic world, we can make more time to be together and relax together as a family.

- In what ways can parents teach their children essential Christian truth?

- How do you go about family devotions? Talk about how you can avoid getting into a rut with them.

- Discuss communication problems within the family and how you go about resolving them.

- What does disciplining involve?

- Do you consider yourselves to be consistent when it comes to disciplining your children?

- Are you a good listener when a child tries to share what they feel or talk about something that's bothering them?

- What, in the light of studying this section on family life, are new goals and aims for your family?

---

# TIL WHAT DO US PART?

## Winifred Ascroft

*Winifred Ascroft is National President of Women's Aglow, the international full Gospel evangelistic ministry with some 60 chapters in England, Scotland and Wales. A mother and a grandmother, Winifred, who is widowed, lives at Tarleton, near Preston. Over the past few years she has seen an increasing need within Women's Aglow to minister to Christian women whose marriages have run into trouble.*

**DAY 1**

**Genesis 1:27, 2:18–25; Mark 10:9**

Marriage is in big trouble today. One in three marriages in Britain finish in divorce and the number is rising. Increasingly, Christians are caught up in this trend. So what is the solution to the problem? How can married couples stay married "til death us do part?" And how can that lifelong union be a happy one?

The blueprint for successful marriage was, in fact, given by God at creation. Wedded couples should live together harmoniously and with mutual affection, providing a loving and stable environment for their children. Such an atmosphere is vital for children to grow up into balanced, secure adults. So the goal of marriage is oneness in spirit, soul and body. Let's begin the search into how this can be achieved.

To create the family unit, husband and wife must leave their parents and cleave (adhere, stick fast) to each other (Matt. 19:5). This doesn't mean that they are to have nothing more to do with their parents – that would go against God's command to honour their father and mother (Mark 7:10). But the relationship with parents is on a different level. Leaving father and mother is not only physical, but emotional and financial as well.

Parents should no longer be relied on to meet these needs. Their counsel may be valuable, but parents should not be relied on to take decisions. The marriage relationship itself must take priority over all other human relationships. There must be willingness and determination to pull together as a team.

 **Lord Jesus, thank you for the gift of marriage. Help those of us who are married, or are contemplating marriage, to follow your blueprint and be truly at one with our partners.**

 *In what ways do you show your partner that he or she is the most important human being in your life?*

*What steps do you need to take to improve the oneness with your husband or wife?*

 **Ephesians 5:22,23; Proverbs 31:10–31**

Everybody has needs. They can be defined as the Triple S. *Security:* the need to be loved. *Significance:* The opportunity to make a meaningful contribution to one's immediate world. *Self-worth:* The need to see ourselves as being valued in the eyes of another person. Often people enter marriage with the mistaken idea that their partner will meet all of their needs. That brings undue pressure on the relationship. Only Jesus can meet our needs.

Jesus is the unfailing source of security (Rom. 5:8), significance (Eph. 2:10) and self-worth (Luke 12:6,7). God loves us and has laid out specific responsibilities for husbands and wives to enable them to have a deep and satisfying love relationship with each other. Husbands are to lovingly assume the responsibilities of headship, loving their wives like Christ loves his Church.

Christ's love is unconditional (1 John 3:16), intense and unending (John 13:1), unselfish (Phil. 2:5–8) and with a servant attitude (John 13:12–14). In praying for us, providing for our needs (8:32), protecting, leading, helping and comforting, Jesus gives a wonderful picture of what a husband-wife relationship should be like.

The wife's responsibility in God's plan is to submit to her

husband. *Submit* is an emotive word today, particularly with militant feminists, but a wife submits to her husband in an act of obedience to God – regardless of what her partner may be doing. A Christian wife who truly loves her husband finds submission a joy rather than a drudgery.

 **Help us, Lord, to fulfil the roles that you have given to us in marriage, not just for our personal happiness and satisfaction, but that we will be a light to those in a society whose relationships are battered, bruised and torn apart.**

 *Husbands: What areas do you need to work on to make your wife feel truly loved and fulfilled?*

*Wives: How submitted are you to your husband and helping to meet his basic need?*

# DAY 3

### 1 Corinthians 13:1–8; Ephesians 4:1–7, 22–32

"All you need is love" goes the song popularised by the Beatles. But what sort of love? Just the romantic moonlight-and-roses kind, with its feelings of excitement and exhilaration? Far more than that is needed for a proper, happy, fulfilled marriage! The kind of love needed is unselfish, as our first passage underlines – a love that seeks to give rather than to get and desires to minister to the other partner's needs.

No relationship can develop unless a couple spend time together, talk with each other and listen to what the other is saying – *really* saying, that is. Listening is not thinking about what you are going to say until the other person has finished speaking! Lack of real communication is a big factor in marriages foundering on the rocks. If a conflict of opinion arises out of what is being said, resolve it quickly (Jas. 4:1–3; Eph. 4:26). The husband, as leader in the home, should take the initiative in seeking a solution. Views need to be aired in love (Eph. 4:15). It may well be necessary to differ, but it will always be important to forgive.

Marriage partners, being each other's best friend, have the responsibility to encourage each other to grow spiritually. Regular study of the Scriptures and daily prayer together are very important in drawing us nearer to the Lord and to each other. It also gives us a basis for communicating on other aspects of our lives.

Sexual relationships and managing the budget are important subjects covered in other sections of this study guide, but however well we work these things out, our marriage will never truly be enriched unless we care about each other's spiritual growth.

 **Heavenly Father, the height and depth of your love for us is overwhelming. Flood us afresh with your Holy Spirit so that we may begin to love as you love.**

 *Do you really listen to what your partner is saying?*

*When marital conflicts occur, do you resolve them quickly and satisfactorily enough? In what ways can you improve on sorting out your differences?*

**Malachi 2:10–17; Hosea 2:19,20**

Sharing a meal is used in the East for sealing a covenant. Similarly, the wedding breakfast signifies a binding contract between two people. They have promised to be faithful to each other for life – "For better or worse, for richer or poorer, in sickness and in health, including bulges, bunions, baldness and bifocals," as someone put it. In effect, the couple making the covenant are saying, "All I have is yours – my name, money, possessions and home. From now on you have a right to them." There is 100 per cent commitment to each other. To live together without marrying, on the other hand, means a lack of deep love and commitment, a fear of trusting oneself and possessions to the other person.

Unfaithfulness cuts a jagged, and often fatal, wound in the marriage relationship. There are other damaging pitfalls and we must be alert when we come across the danger signs. Over-commitment to work or career (and even to church activities) can drive a marriage on to the rocks. A wife can be left at home, by herself or with the children, for long hours feeling lonely, discontented, depressed and angry at her husband's continual long absences and lack of attention.

Selfishness is deadly. People can be put into two categories – givers and takers. A marriage between two givers can be a beautiful thing, but between two takers it is doomed to failure. And friction results in a relationship between a giver and a taker.

Unrealistic expectations of marriage as a blissful, romantic, perfect relationship where one partner expects from the other more than they are able to give themselves inevitably leads to disappointment. Marriages may be made in heaven, but they have to be worked out on earth.

 **I begin to understand afresh, Lord, the solemnity and commitment involved in my marriage vows. Help me to work this out in faithfulness to my marriage partner and increasing stability within our relationship in the coming days.**

 *In what areas do you need to work at to become a real giver in marriage?*

*Do you consider that you have got the correct balance between commitment to your partner and family and other commitments such as work, church and leisure activities? If not, seek to adjust to get that right balance.*

**Mark 10:2–9; Matthew 19:1–9**

The easy availability of divorce has led to the widespread attitude among men and women going into marriage that if it doesn't work out they can opt out. What many who go through divorce don't appreciate beforehand is the emotional devastation that it brings, often accompanied by a deep sense of loss, insecurity and failure. It's a case of out of the frying pan into the fire.

In a report called *Full Circle – the Swinging Sixties*, a group of leading psychologists pointed accusing fingers at lack of discipline, trendy schooling, feminism, escalating divorce rate and the breakdown of family life as marks of that decade. Now we are reaping what was sown then – broken homes, huge rises in crime, particularly violent crime, rape and immorality.

For Christians who have made their marriage vows before God, divorce is a grave step indeed. Yet what are a husband and wife to do when the marriage has so badly broken down that it seems beyond hope? As Lawrence Crabb, a Christian psychologist, states, "If we deeply believe that the Lord is able to work for our good in all circumstances, then no collection of marital setbacks will prompt us to seriously consider divorce."

Sometimes, it seems, we are asked to give up all thought of personal happiness to please our partner. This is often the heartcry of a Christian struggling day in, day out to please an unbelieving partner. But how many are willing to continue only as long as there is something in it for *me*? True love is unconditional – it gives and gives and gives. Yet it is a mistake to take this as being passive in the face of cruelty or unfaithfulness. Confrontation, on occasions, may well be the most loving thing to do.

It is the grace of God which gives us strength to love in such circumstances (2 Cor. 12:9,10), grace which is sufficient to enable us to minister to the partner as unto the Lord, willingly and with an attitude that pleases Him. The mainspring of a person's willingness to continue in an unhappy marriage is that they know God desires it (Ps. 40:8) and He can change it.

 **Help me, Lord, to live unselfishly so that your loveliness is seen in my marriage. May I be more concerned about giving than receiving, delighting above all to do your will.**

 *How do you react to a problem in your marriage – by wanting to opt out or work it out?*

*If you know a couple whose marriage is in difficulty, pray for God to help them to be reconciled and their relationship restored.*

**DAY 6**

**1 Corinthians 7:1–17; Matthew 18:21–35**

I was talking with a couple whose marriage was in deep trouble. The husband had been unfaithful and the wife was utterly woebegone.

"I feel totally insecure and unsure of myself about anything," she cried. As we talked, I sensed in her a grief as great as if her husband had died. Many men and women do, in fact, claim that losing a partner through divorce is more traumatic than loss through death. For on top of the departure of the partner there is deliberate rejection and, often, a turning to someone else.

That particular couple were seeking to put the broken pieces of their marriage back together again. Ahead lay months of rebuilding trust and love. The most urgent needs were for the husband to repent of his betrayal and for the wife to truly forgive him. She needed to realise that her security and self-worth were to be found in Jesus – not in her husband.

There is frequently a lot of deep hurt and emotional pain when we have been offended and even betrayed by someone near to us. However, there are eight steps that can help us come to grips with our own thoughts and truly forgive the offender:

1. Jesus was despised and rejected (Isa. 53:3; Heb. 4:15), so we can be confident that He knows the pain and anguish we are suffering. 2. Deliberately *choose* to forgive and treat that person as though they had not deeply wounded you. 3. Pray for God's blessing on them. 4. Do not allow your mind to dwell on the hurt or continually talk about it. 5.Do not look upon the hurt as devaluing your worth or significance – remember that only Jesus can fulfil those needs of self-worth. 6. Realise that the unfaithful marriage partner has needs – and seek to minister to them. 7. Accept your partner as they are, but look to God to change them as you pray. 8. Meditate on the Scriptures and realise how precious you are to God.

**Thank you, heavenly Father, that because you have forgiven me much I, too, can forgive someone who has deeply hurt me. Thank you that as I respond to you your love reaches out to heal, restore my wounded spirit and make me whole.**

*Ask God to show you any lingering bitterness and unforgiveness towards someone, particularly a marriage partner, and be prepared to let Him deal fully with it.*

*How can you help someone who has been deeply wounded by marital unfaithfulness?*

## DAY 7

**Hebrews 9:11–15; Matthew 19:1–12; 1 Corinthians 7:10,11, 27–39; Romans 7:1–3**

We Christians have something wonderful — a covenant relationship with our heavenly Father. To those who come to Jesus, repent of their sins and receive Him into their hearts, God says that all He has is ours. And marriage is, or should be, a picture of what takes place in the spiritual realm — the entering into a relationship of total commitment and faithfulness. Yet, having said all this, human frailty and sinfulness often makes a mess of God's design and marriages do break down and divorce takes place. Tragically, this is an increasing trend among Christians as well as society at large.

This inevitably raises the question of remarriage of divorced believers. There are conflicting views about this within the Church. Many believe the Scriptures (especially 1 Cor. 7:10,11), counsel against divorcees remarrying while their (former) partner is alive, even when the marriage has ended because their husband or wife has been the offending, adulterous party. Some believe that remarriage is permissible in God's eyes when the failed marriage began before one of the partners became a Christian, if the unbeliever wants to end it.

Many go into a second marriage on the grounds that God's grace covers their frailties and failures. This raises the question of how much we can presume about this without contradicting Scripture — God does forgive the truly repentant, but can this, in fact, be taken as permission to remarry?

Those who go through the fires of divorce need sympathy and understanding. Most of all, they need to know that God's love is unchanging, that He does forgive them for their failure to stay in lifelong union with their marriage partner. When it comes to the question of remarriage, it is their responsibility to seek God with open, rather than pre-conceived, minds about what the Scriptures actually say on the subject. There is also a heavy responsibility laid before church leaders to act Scripturally, rather than emotionally, when divorcees ask to remarry.

 **Lord God, I confess that the question of divorce and remarriage is a perplexing one. Help those who have to face the question of another marriage to hear you clearly speak to them, and give wisdom to Christian leaders who have to decide whether to allow such a marriage to take place.**

---

### FOR GROUP DISCUSSION

● When we marry, we must leave our parents. But how much responsibility should we continue to have for them, especially when they get older?

● The virtuous wife of Proverbs 31:10–31 was given wide scope in her marriage. Why do you think this was?

● In submitting to her husband, do you think she should be mainly looking after the home or is there freedom for her to pursue a career?

● How important is it that those contemplating marriage should only choose a Christian partner, given that Christian women far outnumber Christian men?

● How can one minister to one's partner in a strained relationship, continuing to give and give again and again without becoming too subservient or losing self-respect?

● Is there such a thing as "incompatibility"?

● Opposites attract, but do they work in a marriage relationship?

● Is there ever a truly "innocent party" in a divorce?

● Does Scripture allow for divorced people to remarry?

---

### Suggested further reading

*Marriage as God Intended* Selwyn Hughes (Kingsway)
*Marriage on the Mend* Joyce Huggett
*Second Honeymoon* Dave & Joyce Ames (Kingsway)
*Looking up the Aisle?* Dave & Joyce Ames (Kingsway)
*Marriage – the Early Years* Ian & Ruth Coffey (Kingsway).

# CELEBRATING ONENESS

## Dave & Joyce Ames

*Dave and Joyce Ames have been married for 36 years. They have three children and five grandchildren. In 1975 they began a ministry among American servicemen and women stationed in Britain which resulted in a Christian Servicemen's Centre. Two years later they conducted their first Christian Marriage Weekend, which led to the start of their present ministry, Mission to Marriage. They wrote a book based on those weekends,* Second Honeymoon *(Kingsway). Their most recent book is* Looking Up the Aisle? – A couples' guide to friendship, romance and marriage *(also published by Kingsway). Their Looking Up the Aisle seminars are aimed at equipping churches for marriage preparation.*

**DAY 1**

### Genesis 1:27,28; 2:18–25

"The two shall become one." That certainly speaks of sexual relations, but the Bible never limits itself to one dimension. The fact is that if a couple are not spiritually and psychologically one, physical oneness will become impossible.

God's statement, "It is not good for the man to be alone," makes it sound as if He may have been experimenting and suddenly realised that Adam was lonely. We know better, if for no other reason that all of the qualities of God that He was to pass on to mankind were not present in Adam. For God also has a mother's heart and many other aspects of His nature which are more clearly portrayed in women.

So marriage is a uniting of the complementary characteristics of God which are seen in men and women. Since the basic physical material God used to create Eve came from Adam, marriage is to some degree a *reuniting*.

Sexual intercourse is an acknowledgement of this reunion and a physical demonstration of the oneness they are continually striving towards. Just as baptism and the Lord's

Supper are physical celebrations of spiritual realities, sexual intercourse is also a physical celebration of a spiritual and psychological reality.

 **Lord, we thank you for making us equal, different and complementary, and that you have designed us with the potential to relate with spirit, soul and body.**

 *Does your attitude towards physical relations treat them as something approaching a sacrament or more as a physical urge or appetite?*

*Has the complementary aspect of your relationship deteriorated into competition, to the detriment of your sex life?*

 **Ephesians 5:21–31**

Contrary to popular secular opinion, sexual relations are the celebration of a relationship and not the reason for it. We are sure most Christians agree with that statement, but nevertheless couple after couple experiencing sexual dissatisfaction find that they have lost sight of this basic concept. We are not necessarily guilty of borrowing our sexual ethics from a secular world view, but it seems to be more of a matter of attempting to fit 30 hours into each day.

It may sound harsh, but when this happens we must come to grips with the fact that, more often than not, our own selfishness lies at the bottom of the problem. Life has a lot to offer and we want it all. We want money and the comforts it will provide, a full social life, position, recognition and the opportunity to make a meaningful contribution to society. We also want a happy family which has grown out of a successful marriage which also provides a fulfilling sex life. Some people are talented enough to accomplish all this, but most of us have to choose what to go for.

An unsatisfying sex life may indicate that our marriage is suffering from a faulty priority system. We somehow expect that we can allow a crowded schedule to erode the quantity and quality of the time we spend together and still experience a satisfying sex life. So we find that we are actually attempting to participate in the celebration of a relationship which is virtually non-existent.

 Heavenly Father, grant that I may never enter into the act of marriage for anything other than to celebrate the state of the relationship with the partner you have so graciously provided.

 *Is the quality of your relationship with your husband or wife actually anything to celebrate?*

*What can you do to bring cause for celebration?*

**Matthew 5:23, 24; 18:15**

It is not too difficult to make some correlation between the quality of our communication and the quality of our sexual relations. The Bible speaks specifically about the most common barrier to fulfilling sexual relations, which is indeed a communication problem. It is resentment which arises from hurts and irritations that aren't properly dealt with.

It is probably because Proverbs speaks of the virtues of overlooking an offence (17:9; 19:11), that we seem to think it more spiritual just to keep a lid on our emotions. When, however, we obviously don't have the grace to overlook a particular offence, we should see that as a sign that it is something that shouldn't be ignored. A confrontation is in order. Certainly we can't just go in with guns blazing, but carefully work out the least offensive approach. After all, we are attempting to heal a relationship, not win a victory.

This is where phrases such as "I have a problem I think you can help me with" come in handy. Conversely, there will be times when we realise that we have offended our partner and need to be equally motivated to go to them and put it right. God demands it.

 Lord, please do not let my desire for peace and tranquillity allow me to ignore my responsibility to my marriage. Give me the wisdom and creative insight to broach sensitive issues and not leave it for my partner to deal with.

*Are you attempting to overlook more than you have the grace to overlook because you lack the courage to confront your partner?*

*Do you make yourself easy to approach or would your partner find a confrontation with you a daunting prospect?*

 **Proverbs 5:15–19; Song of Songs 1:12–2:4**

Procreation is an obvious purpose for sex, but so is pleasure. The very fact that sex continues to bring pleasure in a healthy marriage long after child-bearing years should speak volumes in itself. Scripture reflects this all the way through. Dr Ed Wheat in *Intended for Pleasure* sees Proverbs 5 this way, "The ancient counsel given by father to son, based upon the wisdom of God in Proverbs 5:18,19 comes across just as clearly to the reader of today: 'Let your fountain [your body parts which produce life] be blessed, and rejoice [or ecstatically delight] with the wife of your youth. Let her breasts satisfy you at all times, and be ravished [or filled] with her love."

The problem is that mankind is easily drawn into sexual expressions which are plain selfishness. When one individual satisfies himself at the expense of another, it can be terrifying — if not traumatic. Some people fear self-gratification is what is meant by sexual pleasure and, therefore, conclude that God never intended anything but procreation.

Others claim the Song of Songs is not a commentary on married sexual love but merely an allegory about Christ's relationship to the Church. Yet would God use something abnormal or sinful to portray His truth? We find it interesting that the apostle Paul, looking for a parallel to Christ's relationship with the Church, chose Genesis 2:4 — "The two will become one flesh." If a celibate wasn't afraid to compare the intimacy of marriage with Christ's relationship to the Church, sexual pleasure in marriage was most likely normal, common knowledge and much more easy to discuss than it is today.

 **Lord, thank you for the gift of sexual relations with my marriage partner.**

*Are you benefiting from God's gift?*

*Have you allowed Satan to distort God's purposes for sex?*

**1 Corinthians 7:3–5**

This is probably the most important passage in our Christian view of sexual relations. It is obviously not considering procreation, which is one more proof that God also intends sex for pleasure. The passage has been used to establish "conjugal rights", but as with any issue of so-called "rights", the Bible turns the focus on to responsibilities.

The Christian perspective on human rights has always been the protection of others, not simply to claim our own rights. And sexual relations is no exception. Secular society says, "I have a right to have *my* sexual needs met." The Christian's priority should be to meet their partner's needs. It is totally opposite to the spirit of the age because it changes the emphasis from getting to giving.

And this is actually the guarantee to sexual satisfaction. When people concentrate on their own pleasure, fulfilment eludes them. Self-centred searching for gratification sometimes leads to experimentation with bizarre and exotic paraphernalia and unusual techniques which leave all concerned with a distorted picture of sex. Freedom and fulfilment only comes when we concentrate on pleasing our marriage partner. That's what real love is – a commitment to doing the very best for the person we love. And that type of love is the most fulfilling.

**Heavenly Father, help me to trust you and your plan and not be side-tracked by the spirit of the age. Help to keep my focus on my partner's fulfilment.**

*Examine your thought life and honestly ask yourself: Do I honestly put my partner's pleasure first?*

*Have you introduced anything into our sexual relations which is geared solely toward satisfying yourself?*

**Matthew 5:27–30**

"Society has sex on the brain," declared Malcolm Muggeridge, adding that it "is a very uncomfortable place to have it." This means that anyone who values God's standards, his or her marriage partner and personal integrity is battling against sexual immorality and infidelity on an unprecedented scale.

In a previous chapter of this study guide it was stated that "unfaithfulness cuts a jagged, and often fatal, wound in the marriage relationship." This is probably the single most avoidable wound of married life, for adultery is always self-inflicted. It doesn't lie like a spring-loaded animal trap, cocked and waiting for us to walk slap into it, but is more like planning a holiday because it involves many decisions and numerous opportunities to back out.

Unfaithfulness doesn't begin with the actual physical act nor by setting up a secret rendezvous and lying to our husband or wife about where we will be at that particular time. It doesn't even start with being sexually attracted to another man or woman or not finding our partner desirable any more. It *does* begin when we allow ourselves to entertain romantic or sexual thoughts which do not include our partner.

Jesus says that an attitude of adultery is as bad as the physical act. Which means that the greatest safeguard against unfaithfulness is for husbands and wives to make a commitment never to think romantically or sexually about anyone but their partner.

 **Lord, help me to rid myself of sexual thoughts that cater only for my own selfishness and to put on thoughts which enhance my marriage.**

 *Do you actually need to make a commitment to God never to think romantically or sexually about anyone but your husband/wife?*

*Are you involved in any relationship which is placing you under undue temptation?*

**Exodus 20:14**

The Bible introduces sex, celebrates sex and limits sex. Many in today's society rebel against any limitations on sex, dismissing them as intolerable, dictatorial, austere and old-fashioned. But God's commands were all designed to ensure quality of life, not make life more complicated. His limitations on sex are positive, aimed at making physical relations the most special and unique expression of love and trust a human being can bestow on another.

In that relationship each partner makes themselves pretty vulnerable because they totally trust their mate with something very important. Sexual relations not only allow each partner to become familiar with the most protected parts of their bodies, but also expose their very souls. This is in stark contrast to the way we conduct ourselves all day long in a very competitive society.

Sexual relations allow each partner to remove their emotional armour. With no limitations, however, that vulnerability can be lost. Sex then becomes a performance, with fears that one's body is being compared with other lovers. Everything is devalued. How much would we respect a Victoria Cross if one came in every packet of cornflakes?

 **Lord, thank you that, in your wisdom, you have given us principles to guard against misuse of the gifts you have given us.**

## FOR GROUP DISCUSSION

● Does the fact that God said "It is not good for the man to be alone" and made "a suitable helper" capable of entering into sexual relations give any priority to such relations?

● What do you think of the comparing of sexual relations with baptism and communion?

● What does the statement, "Sexual relations are the celebration of a relationship and not the reason for it" say to you? What responsibility does it convey?

● How can a couple protect their relationship from the often frenetic pace of life?

● How do we balance Proverbs 17:9 and 19:11 (overlooking an offence) against Matthew 18:15 (confrontation)?

● In what ways would you help a friend who has grown up with a fairly prudish attitude towards sexual relations to see God's perspective on the subject?

● How could the 1 Corinthians 7:3–5 passage be used to show whether or not a particular sexual practice is acceptable when the Bible doesn't mention it specifically?

● Do you believe that men are tempted to unfaithfulness by different situations than women? Discuss what the primary causes are and the best way to deal with temptation.

● Recent surveys show that only four per cent of people in Britain think the Church is a good source of sexual information — despite the fact that Christians have the Maker's manual. Why do you think this is? Is your church giving full Biblical teaching on sex?

### Suggested further reading

*Second Honeymoon* Dave & Joyce Ames (Kingsway)
*Looking Up the Aisle?* Dave & Joyce Ames (Kingsway)
*Intended for Pleasure* Ed & Gaye Wheat (Scripture Union).

# MONEY MATTERS

## Winifred Ascroft

**DAY 1**

**Matthew 6:19–34; 13:44–46**

"Take my silver and my gold, not a mite would I withhold," we happily sing at church. But do we really mean it? "After all," we rationalize, "for someone on such a small wage, God surely can't expect me to give any more – I need it." The problem is that we often use the same argument after substantial rises. Jesus taught about money and giving on numerous occasions during His earthly ministry. As we study the principles, we might be forgiven for thinking that we are with Alice in Wonderland at the place where everything was upside down and people walked on the ceiling instead of the floor!

So much of what Jesus taught about money is revolutionary compared with the world's philosophy, which amounts to getting as much as you can, spend it all on yourself and the more you have the happier you will be. For our Lord taught that it was more blessed to *give* than to receive, heavenly treasure is much more important than earthly treasure and that if we are to truly be His disciples we must be willing to give up everything and follow Him (Luke 14:33). One man who gave up fame and a fortune was Charles (C.T.) Studd. He exchanged a large financial inheritance and career as an England cricketer for the far greater rewards of serving Christ in China, India and the Belgian Congo (now Zaïre).

Jesus himself set us an example by leaving His heavenly majesty and exchanging His riches for poverty (2 Cor. 8:9). He became a servant (Phil. 2:6–9), went hungry on occasions (Mark 6:31), had little or no privacy (Matt. 14:13) and finally gave up His life on a cross (John 10:15–17). As we meditate on the extent of His giving to us, surely our response must be to give ourselves to Him (2 Cor. 5:14,15).

**Lord Jesus, I begin to realise how much it cost you to send Jesus to be my Saviour. I see that everything I have comes from you. By your grace help me to give myself and all that I have in full and glad surrender to you.**

 *How much grip does the Lord Jesus have on your finances?*

*Does the Kingdom of God benefit by your pay rises?*

**Matthew 25:31–40; Luke 12:16–21; 19:1–10**

There are three conversions necessary, according to Martin Luther – heart, mind and pocket. A proof of our commitment to Jesus is a change in our attitude to possessions as well as transformation of our heart and mind. Money is not a neutral force, as some would think, points out Richard Foster in his book, *Money, Sex and Power*. It has a personal and spiritual character. That's why Jesus identified mammon as a rival god having a power that seeks to dominate us and cause us to worship it.

Money, adored in that way, belongs to the principalities and powers of darkness described in Ephesians 6:12. No wonder Jesus said that we cannot serve God *and* money (Luke 16:13).

For the average man (and woman) in the street, money is a symbol of status and power. Those who have a lot of it have a lot of significance and security. This mistaken belief leads to a desire for more and more of it at any cost. Yet Jesus said this was foolish. That's why He exhorted us to "seek first his kingdom and his righteousness, and all these things will be given to you as well" (Matt. 6:37).

In this increasingly materialistic age dominated by the stock market and spend-spend-spend-with-little-plastic-friend(s), we Christians need to remember that money should be our servant, not our master, and use it to extend the Kingdom of God rather than lavish it on luxuries for ourselves.

 **Help me, Lord, to take your view of money, so that it will never be an object of my worship but may be a servant which can be used to benefit the extension of your Kingdom.**

*Where does your security lie?*

*What is your attitude to credit cards?*

**DAY 3**

**1 Timothy 6:6–19; 2 Corinthians 8:7–21**

God's normal way of supplying our needs and putting money in our pockets and purses is through using the health and strength He has given us in honest work. Laziness is not encouraged or approved anywhere in the Bible (2 Thess. 3:10; John 5:17). Usually our work is rewarded by some measure of prosperity (Prov. 10:4; Eph. 4:28). It is good to remember that a house to live in, clothes on our backs and food to eat makes us rich compared with two thirds of the world's population!

Someone got it just about right when they said, "Gain all you can, save all you can, give all you can." Saving is important (Prov. 21:20) and it is a Christian responsibility to do so for the family (1 Tim. 5:8) and, possibly, to provide for when we retire from daily work. Yet, at the same time, we must not use those responsibilities as an excuse not to serve God, as Jesus clearly taught (Luke 9:57–62).

"We have clear indications that money in the Christian life is made in order to give it away," said Jacque Ellol. John Wesley had definite views about money, teaching Christians to give away all that wasn't necessary. Plain, wholesome food, clean clothes and enough money to carry on one's business was sufficient in his estimation. At the height of his ministry, he earned £1,400 a year from writing books, a fortune in those 18th century days, but he continued to live on £30 a year and gave away the rest.

We Christians of the late 20th century are called to live a simple lifestyle, not to covet this world's goods but to be willing to share with people who are less well off than ourselves.

 **Help me to be willing, Lord, to give and not count the cost, to have a simpler lifestyle for the love of Jesus. Help me not to be squeezed into the world's mould and fashion, but give me your mind and attitude.**

*Do a mental review of your income, spending, savings and giving. Is there room for adjustment?*

*Is there any unnecessary spending you can cut out and use that money for God's purpose?*

## DAY 4

Deuteronomy 26:12–15; Malachi 3:7–12; Mark 12:41–44

We are realising that Christians are to have a different attitude to money than the world. But living in a society that bases its economy on hard cash rather than the barter system of earlier days, we have to use money to buy food and clothes, as well as keep a roof over our heads. So how do we begin to divide our income and use it in ways that please God?

Both the Old and New Testaments give the yardstick: the tithe. This provides a sound starting point at which to begin our giving to the Lord. Moses was told by God that the children of Israel were to offer Him the first fruits from their trees, grain and cattle (Lev. 27:30–32). The priests were to be paid out of that offering – it was their only source of income. In other words, the tithe was used to support those in full-time ministry. This ministry of building God's kingdom was taught by both Jesus and the apostle Paul (Luke 10:7; 1 Tim. 6:18).

The tithe is a tenth of the gross income. As we tithe, God promises to bless (Prov. 3:9,10; 11:25). As well as the tithe, additional offerings were called for (Lev. 19:9,10; Deut. 14:28,29; Ex. 25:1–8).

Giving a graduated tithe is a suggestion from Ron Sider. By this a modest standard of living is decided upon and 10 per cent of it is tithed. Out of every £500 of additional income five per cent is added to the tithe and once £10,000 is reached, all additional income is given away. Tithing increases trust in God and our dependence on Him, making us less dependent on material possessions.

**May your Kingdom come in our land today, Lord. Touch the hearts of your people so that finances will be released to fund local and national evangelism.**

*What is the basis for your giving to God?*

*Do you give cheerfully or reluctantly for His service?*

**Luke 14:28–30; Romans 13:6–8**

We live in a world of spend, spend, spend and buy now, pay later. This makes it so easy to become engulfed in huge debts through getting more goods with our credit cards than we could afford, or having a bank loan which turns out to be far tougher to pay back than we envisaged. We Christians have a responsibility to live within our means and not get into debt. To write cheques when the bank account is empty, claiming that God will miraculously provide for our wants, is sheer presumption most of the time. A bounced cheque is a bad witness.

God *does* promise to supply all our needs (Phil. 4:19), but it is often our greed that causes the problems. The only way to avoid the debt trap is to set our faces against overspending and ask God to help us plan our finances (2 Cor. 9:8)

Here's one approach to this: 1. Assess what your income is. 2. Determine to give your tithe to the Lord. 3. Set aside money to pay taxes, if they are not automatically deducted (Mark 12:17). 4. Work out the various needs – mortgage or rent, community charge, heating, lighting, food and clothes, telephone, car, holidays, birthday and Christmas gifts. Have an emergency fund for large repair bills for the car, cooker and heating system. Make a savings plan, too – it is better to save up and pay cash than to pay high interest rates wherever it is possible.

The wonderful thing is that we are not alone in the struggle to make ends meet. We can, as the old hymn says, "take it to the Lord in prayer" (James 5:16; Prov. 3:5,6).

 **Thank you, heavenly Father, that you have promised to supply all our needs – not just financial, but emotional and spiritual as well. Help me to trust you more and bring every need to you in prayer.**

 *How do you tell the difference between a need and a want?*

*Do you have a plan to safeguard against your spending exceeding your income?*

**DAY 6**

**Matthew 19:16–30; Luke 12:15–21; Philippians 4:11,12**

To be or not to be? Wealthy, that is. There were wealthy people in the Old and New Testaments. People like Abraham (Gen.13:2), Isaac (Gen. 26:12-14) and Job (Job 1:1-3;42:10) were the equivalent of today's multi-millionaires. They were righteous — men who lived for God and their riches were a blessing from Him. Wealth is not wrong in itself — it's our attitude towards it which counts, as Jesus emphasised in our first two readings today.

Our Lord could see that the rich young man's fortune was a barrier to serving Him wholeheartedly, which is why He challenged him to give it all away. Not every rich person has to do that, for they will want to serve God by investing their earthly wealth in His eternal purposes rather than lavish it on themselves in a life of self-indulgence and ease.

The missionary or evangelist may have been at the sharp end of an important move of God to proclaim the Good News of His Son, but it has been the largely unseen support of individual wealthy believers who have played a vital role in supplying the necessary funds in numerous cases down the years.

When we invest in God's kingdom He does prosper us — but not always financially. Many of us, if we are honest enough to admit it, would lose out spiritually if we had huge amounts of money (Deut. 8:11–14).

 **Help me, Lord, not to crave for the riches of this world, the things that will perish, but give me a hunger for the riches of your Kingdom.**

 *How much does a love of the world and its riches hinder our spiritual growth?*

*List some of the ways God has prospered you other than financially. What special answers to prayer have you received which have made you realise that He is watching over you?*

**DAY 7**

**2 Corinthians 8:1–9; 9:1–13; Matthew 6:1–3**

It was George Verwer, founder and International Co-ordinator of Operation Mobilisation, who pointed out that a lot of Christian work is being severely hampered by lack of financial support from the body of Christ. The need for cheerful, enthusiastic, generous-hearted believers to give cash for the cause of the Kingdom has never been greater or more urgent than it is now!

Giving to missions, missionaries, for the translation and printing of the Scriptures in other languages, disaster relief and medical aid is not just the responsibility of the comparatively few rich Christians, either – we are all called to play a part.

A striking example of this kind of giving is recorded in our first passage today. The Church in Macedonia, though materially poorly off, gladly gave to help others in need. They gave *liberally* (v.2), *voluntarily* and *sacrificially* (v.3), and *prayerfully* (v.5). Those Christians had learned the secret of regular, disciplined giving (1 Cor. 16:2), so that when special needs arose they responded willingly and joyfully (2 Cor. 8:16,17; 9:7).

 **Lord, I now see the importance of giving so that your work throughout this world will not be hindered. Help me to adjust my lifestyle so that I can give as you want me to for the reaping of the spiritual harvest.**

---

### FOR GROUP DISCUSSION

● Do you accept the tithing principle?

● What about those with heavy family responsibilities – do you think tithing is right for them?

● Have you any alternative methods of giving to the Lord?

● How much of your giving should, in your opinion, be (a) to the local church and (b) to other Christian work?

● Is it right to run up interest charges for goods purchased?

● How can an unemployed person give to the Lord?

# HELP! I'M GETTING OLDER!

## Rita McLaughlan

*Rita McLaughlan has written for CWR publications over the past few years, especially* Young People's EDWJ *and* The Life of Christ. *The mother of two sons and two daughters (all either grown up or nearly grown up), she is involved with Holywell Christian Fellowship in Watford, as well as the local Lydia women's intercessory prayer group.*

## DAY 1

**Isaiah 40:6–8; Psalm 90:10; 1 Corinthians 15:39–58**

As I peer through my bifocals to write these studies and reflect that if I have to hurry to catch the post my teenage son can get to the pillar box in half the time it would take me, I am very conscious that "all flesh is as grass." Ageing is an inevitable process, although one which most of us don't look forward to with any great enthusiasm. Flesh and blood gradually deteriorates over the years. Hair turns grey, skin wrinkles, bones ache and eyesight changes.

But the great news for Christians is that after the natural body dies we will be raised up with a spiritual body to be with Him in His kingdom for eternity.

In the meantime, how can we cope with the changes as we grow older and the difficulties of old age? What should our attitude be towards the elderly and towards our own latter years? Look again at 1 Corinthians 15:58. How positive it is! The apostle Paul has been writing about the glorious victory of death, but he comes back to the practicalities of life on earth – "Always give yourselves fully to the work of the Lord." That means at any age, whatever you feel like, however weak you may be and whatever you may have accomplished in the past – always.

God has a purpose for everyone who belongs to Him, a purpose for every day of our lives whether they be long or short. When God told Moses to take a census of the people (Numbers 1:2), he placed no upper age limit on those called to serve in the army (vs 3). Each day we are given is for giving, serving and for living to the full.

 **Dear Father, please help me to live each day of my life according to your will.**

 *What is my attitude to old age? What would I like to have accomplished 10 years from now?*

*Look again at Isaiah 40:8 and 1 Corinthians 15:58. What do you sense God is saying to you through those verses?*

## DAY 2

**Joshua 13:1; 14:6–15**

Neither Joshua nor Caleb thought it was time to retire and take things easy because they were getting on in years! They weren't daunted by the mammoth task facing them – there was work to be done and they were eager to get on with it. Caleb had always been positive and optimistic (Num. 13:30), with unshakeable faith in the Lord. God had promised him an inheritance in Canaan (Num. 14:24) and, at 85, the old warrior was prepared to do battle to possess it.

You might have thought he would settle for something easier at his age, like a cottage beside the Jordan! Not Caleb. He went for the hill country ruled by giants in fortified cities. Caleb knew he could conquer because he knew his God through many years of serving Him wholeheartedly. God had promised him the prized Hebron, God had kept him alive to see that promise fulfilled, God had given him the strength for the task. So Caleb was afraid of nothing.

What lessons to learn from this! Caleb never lost sight of God's promise in 45 years of marching and counter-marching across the desert as the Lord judged Israel for their unbelief in being able, through Him, to take possession of the promised land (Num. 13:31—14:3). We sometimes forget God's promises, especially through the dark clouds of adverse circumstances, but He never forgets them. The promise to Caleb, however, didn't fall into his lap – he had to fight to see its fulfilment. Another lesson is that, even at the advanced age of 85, Caleb was prepared to accept new challenges, new situations, new opportunities.

 **Father God, thank you for keeping me alive until now. I now lay hold of your promises and accept your challenges.**

 *Are there any unfulfilled promises in your life? Are you holding on to them, ready to act when God directs?*

*Maybe adverse circumstances and the passing of time have caused you to doubt God's promises to you. If so, ask Him to give you a new vision of His purposes for your life as you recommit yourself wholeheartedly to Him.*

## DAY 3

**Isaiah 40:28–31; 46:3,4; Psalm 18:28–36; Philippians 4:12,13**

It is God who gives us strength. This is just as true in old age as it is in our youth. So many Christians try to serve the Lord in their own strength and eventually fall. The elderly have a distinct advantage here – they haven't got so much of their own strength to rely upon and quickly realise how frail human flesh is. God understands us, knows what we are capable of and will always give us the ability, strength and staying power to accomplish what He wants us to do. When we accept our limitations and totally rely on Him, He can use us in ways that we probably haven't thought of.

Catherine Bramwell-Booth, granddaughter of William Booth, founder of the Salvation Army, wrote when she had been in retirement for 30 years, "It rushed over me, the thought that I was no good, too old, nobody wanted me any more. I had a conversation with God: 'Help me to accept the fact of old age. It's your ordinance, Lord. I haven't got the physical gumption in me any more.'" The next day she was asked to do a TV interview – a door which led to many more interviews and broadcasts in which she challenged millions with her direct approach to the Gospel.

Accept yourself for who you are, what you are, where you are. Be honest with yourself and with God about what you can and cannot do – you'll be surprised with what *He* can do through you.

**Lord, help me now to accept myself as you accept me and lean on you trustfully for the strength I need for every day.**

 *List any personal physical or mental weaknesses and then read 2 Corinthians 12:9,10.*

*What positive promises has God given you through today's readings. Are there any conditions to them?*

### Luke 1:8–20; 2:36–38; 13:10–16

Three elderly people in very different circumstances. Yet each had one thing in common — they were crippled. Zechariah was crippled by doubt. He thought his age was a barrier to the fulfilment of the angel's prophecy and was struck dumb for his unbelief. But that was only a temporary measure – until God had demonstrated that age is no problem to Him by fulfilling that prophecy and presenting an overjoyed elderly couple with a child. God's miracle-working power overcomes our human frailties.

Anna was a widow – and that meant, in the Israel of those days, extreme poverty and deprivation. She had been a widow since she was a young woman, yet she had not let it cripple her. She put herself and her time at God's disposal to become a prophetess and an intercessor. What a reward she received! She recognised the Saviour of the world and spread the good news about Him. God is calling His people to be intercessors today – and it's a ministry many elderly people can, and do, take up.

We are not told exactly how old the bent and crippled lady was, but she must have appeared to be pretty ancient. When Jesus set her free she straightened up immediately and praised God. Though our bodies may age and wear out through the passing of the years, healing and deliverance are available to all – young, middle-aged and old. Circumstances, attitudes, physical illness, demonic influence can cripple us if we allow them to do so, but Jesus can set us free. And He wants to set us free!

 **Lord Jesus, set me free from anything which is holding me back from being what you want me to be.**

*Ask yourself: What is crippling me, holding me back from allowing God to glorify Himself in my life?*

*Ask the Lord to show you what your special responsibilities in prayer and intercession are. How can you spend a regular time in this ministry?*

## DAY 5

### Mark 1:16–20; Luke 9:52–56; Revelation 1:1–3, 9–11

"Sons of Thunder" Jesus called John and James when they were young (Mark 3:17), and their fiery reaction to the inhospitable Samaritan village shows that they were well named. The Galilean fishermen had a reputation for toughness and plain speaking. But John changed. His experiences over the years and his utter devotion to his beloved Lord mellowed his character to such an extent that he was able to write, "God is love. Whoever lives in love lives in God and God in him" (1 John 4:16).

John was already an old man when he wrote his gospel around AD 90. He remembered and recorded Jesus' prayer before his arrest (John ch. 17) and his moving account of the trial and crucifixion must have touched millions of lives down the centuries. Yet it was not just John's accurate memory of events that happened 60 years previously that makes his gospel so moving. His insight into the meaning of it all is the fruit of a life spent walking close to God and allowing the Holy Spirit to not only change him, but to reveal hidden truths for our benefit.

Finally God chose John, by then a very old man exiled on the isle of Patmos, to receive and record for future generations the climax of the ages. John might have thought his usefulness was finished when he arrived on Patmos, but God had saved the best until last!

**Thank you, Heavenly Father, for all you have done for me and shown me over the years. Please use me in your service in any way you want.**

*Looking back to when you first gave your life to Jesus, how has He changed you?*

*In the light of Psalm 139:23, 24 and 2 Corinthians 3:17, 18, what still needs to be changed or put right?*

**2 Samuel 19:32–38; Psalm 23:1–6**

Move or stay put? Many people nearing retirement age face this question. A picturesque cottage in the country, a bungalow by the sea? Either can seem attractive at 60 when you are fit, active and able to get about easily, but not so practical at 75 or 80 when gales and snowstorms stop you getting to the shops and prevent help arriving quickly. Later on, you may face having to either move in with younger relatives or go into a retirement or nursing home.

Barzillai had a choice. At first glance, King David's offer was very tempting. He had served David well for much of his life and now the king wanted to repay his servant by looking after him in his twilight years. Barzillai carefully weighed up the pros and cons – and decided against it. He had no taste for royal food, was hard of hearing and couldn't see very well. He would be much happier in simpler, familiar surroundings among his own family and friends. David understood and let him go home to end his days there.

For some of us, there may be no choice and we must be content with staying where we are. But for others, after weighing up all the practicalities, the ultimate question must surely be, "Lord, where do you want me to spend the closing days of my life? Where can I be most useful to you now?" For there is no retirement in the Lord's service. We may be less active, even lay down some of our responsibilities – but we are still important to Him. God has a purpose for each one of His servants until the day we die.

 **Lord, please show me exactly where you want me to be at every stage of my life.**

 *Make a note of some practical considerations you may need to take into account in your later years.*

*Take time to consider how and where you can best serve the Lord. Ask Him to clearly show you.*

**John 21:18; Philippians 2:1–11; 1 Peter 5:6, 7**

It's not easy being dependent on others. The most frustrating thing for many old people is having to accept help from younger folk. Yet it can be a most rewarding time spiritually to "humble yourself under God's mighty hand." Jesus set us an example of humility when He came down to earth and limited Himself for a time to human form. On the Cross He made Himself completely helpless for our sakes. Think about that when you feel helpless and frustrated – Jesus understands exactly how you feel. He will comfort and strengthen you as you cast all anxieties on Him.

Also know that your asking for help can be a blessing to others. Young people are often keen to help but don't know how. The chance to do your shopping, help you across the road or just sit and talk for a while will make them feel useful, wanted and appreciated in a world where, sadly, they sometimes don't feel any of these things.

Our latter years are so important to God, such an opportunity to go on learning from Him, serving Him in new ways and, above all, worshipping, loving, praising and thanking Him for who He is and for all He has done.

 **Lord, grant me humility, the ability to accept what I cannot change and a heart to praise you in all circumstances.**

---

## FOR GROUP DISCUSSION

● Study Philippians 3:12–16. How do these verses apply particularly to the elderly?

● What do you think are the most common problems older people face? Physical disability, frustration, feeling useless, loneliness, self-pity – or others?

● How can we Christians guard against these problems in our own lives and help others to overcome them?

● What has God been saying in particular to you through studying this section?

● How do you feel you can serve God effectively once you reach the society's retirement age of 65 for men and 60 for women?

● What do you feel God is calling you to do in the next few years?

---

### Suggested further reading

*The Last Lap* John Eddison (Kingsway)
*Getting Older* Una Kroll (Collins Fount)
*Commissioner Catherine* Catherine Bramwell-Booth (Darton, Longman & Todd)
*Tramp for the Lord* Corrie Ten Boom (Hodder & Stoughton)
*Strengthening Your Grip* (chapter 8) Charles Swindoll (Hodder & Stoughton).

# WHY ME, LORD?

## Sheila Groves

*Sheila Groves was widowed 11 years ago. Apart from being Mum to Tom (13) and Elly (11), she is a freelance writer (regularly contributing to* Young People's Every Day with Jesus), *presenter for Radio Devon and a primary school governor. A member of Otterdale Community Church, she likes walking, reading, theatre, music and making resolutions to learn to draw and finish her novel!*

**DAY 1**

### Job 5:6–19; 1 Corinthians 15:12–22,35–57

Death, it seems, always catches us unawares. Even if someone is elderly or has suffered for a long time, nothing can prepare us for the agony of their absence. Death always seems somehow to be wrong. That's because it *is*. Death screams at us that we live in a world that it is out of key – it was never part of God's original plan, so we are right to see it as an intruder. The same goes for suffering. Nevertheless, since man chose to ignore God, death and suffering are inevitable parts of life for everyone, as we read in Job.

"Why me?" is a common and understandable reaction to tragedy. Yet a more reasonable one is "Why not me?" For no one, not even the Christian, is exempt from suffering and death. When it happens it's hard to believe that you're not totally alone – the rest of the world seems to carry on regardless, unknowing, uncaring.

Christians have one crucial advantage – a new perspective. When my husband died I was horribly afraid that my belief in life after death would prove to be mere wishful thinking. In fact, the reverse was true – tentative faith became certain hope. I could echo the apostle Paul that, thanks to Jesus, death is swallowed up in the victory of new life. Our time on earth is simply a prelude to eternity. To see it in that light does not prevent grief – nor should it – but it does put it into a right and hope-full perspective.

The fact that you have not been singled out to suffer

and the eternal perspective are important factors. A third is a willingness to believe that God *can* heal and restore — *willingness* rather than *belief* because numbness and shock often make it hard to think or believe anything clearly. God needs only our willingness to be able to work, even in the midst of the greatest tragedy.

 **Lord, in times of grief and suffering I can hardly put two thoughts together, let alone pray. But I *am* willing for you to come in and work. Day by day renew my thinking and perspective — and heal and restore me.**

 *"Why me?" "What have I done to deserve this?" Look up John 11:40; 1 Pet. 4:12,13; 2 Cor. 4:16–18; Rom. 8:16,17.*

*How do we know God wants to heal and restore? (See Isa. 61:1–4; 1 Pet. 5:7; Ps. 10:14; 34:18,19).*

### DAY 2

**Psalm 23:1–6; 42:1–11; 1 Corinthians 10:13**

The death of a husband or wife causes the greatest stress. It is too vast, too devastating to take in and numbness and disbelief may last quite a while before grief breaks through. Grief is both natural and necessary. There is a "time to weep ... a time to mourn" (Eccl. 3:4), yet there are also no time limits on grief. It is a "slow, dark, wordless process" as Ann Lindbergh put it. Time, contrary to the popular saying, does *not* heal — only eternity can. True, the pain will not be as intense or constant after a while, but the absence continues to be as real.

Different situations and incidents may bring tears for a long, long time. There's nothing wrong in this — it is only natural for a person who was so precious. Only when grief becomes indulgent self-pity and comfort is refused should a wise counsellor step in. For friends wanting to help, practical love needs to come first — to weep with those who weep (Rom. 12:15) should be taken literally! Listening to a bereaved person is so important, for they must be given the opportunity to talk, especially about the one who has died. It does no good at all to ring up and say, "If I can do anything, let me know." Go round, see for yourself what needs to be done and get on with it. Such a visit may mean intercepting unwanted 'phone calls.

Bereavement is definitely a time for friends and fellow Christians to ask God to deal with any reserve or embarrassment. Be ready to show your love with sensitivity – don't pass by on the other side when a good hug is needed!

It is also important to build up hope in God. Death has shattered a bereaved person's world – life will never be the same again. But God's character has *not* changed, nor has His steadfast love. The Psalms are brilliant in such situations, reflecting a confidence in God in the midst of despair. Many grief-stricken people have found that God has shown His love and care for them in so many ways that they could not doubt Him – despite the "Why?" which often hangs over the loss.

**Father God, thank you for all the signs of your continuing love and care for me. My emotions may be in turmoil and there is much I don't understand, but I trust you – for the present and the future.**

*In the light of Ephesians 6:10 and Galatians 6:2, is it right to try to be self-controlled and cope?*

*What can you do about the fears and panic that so often creep in? (See Matt. 6:34; Prov. 3:5,6; Ps. 27:1–14; Isa. 54:10).*

**Isaiah 53:1–12; 63:9; Luke 7:11–15**

The more we are convinced of God's love for us and His power to heal, the harder it can be to understand why the one we love was not healed. "Jesus healed the widow's son, so why not mine?" you may ask. So many "Why?" demands must remain unanswered. There is a point where understanding must give way to faith. That can be a hard step – especially if it is the first severe test of our faith – but a crucial one. The one thing above everything else that enables us to take this step is the knowledge that Jesus identifies with us in our suffering.

But how? Every situation is different. The death of a

child at birth, a teenager killed in a car crash, the passing away of a parent or a marriage partner after many years together. Jesus never married and never had children, yet the Bible tells us that in all our afflictions He was afflicted. Being God, Jesus not only has the ability to totally enter into and understand other people's situations, but how they *feel* (Heb. 4:15). He is truly the wounded healer.

Sorrow, anger, emptiness, frustration, helplessness, confusion, pointlessness – Jesus understands them all. There is no need to hide such feelings or be ashamed of them, so give them to the Lord and He can (gradually, maybe) transform them.

Guilt often comes in when someone dies. "If only I had checked the cot ... kept my temper ... been more patient ... shown more love ..." Remember – there is nothing God cannot forgive. If we find it hard to forgive ourselves, a good dose of Romans chapter 8 may be needed (just verse 1 will do for a start, if Bible reading is still too hard). God never condemns – it is Satan who accuses us and we must resist him with the truth of what Jesus accomplished for us on the Cross.

 **Lord Jesus, thank you that you fully understand every grief and heartache I experience. Help me to trust in your loving purposes.**

 *Can God really understand the anguish of a parent at the death of their child? (Look up Isa. 49:14–16).*

*Is it possible for a child to come to terms with the death of a parent (See Ps. 62:1–12; 68:5).*

 **Jeremiah 29:10–13; Matthew 26:36–46; 1 Corinthians 7:25–35**

Archbishop Lang has been reported as saying that his great need was not for friends, of whom he had plenty, any more than it was for work, of which he had too much. It was for "that old, simple human thing – someone in daily nearness to love." Many, many people can echo his words, for being single can be tough. The Scriptures themselves have very little to say about singleness, apart from Paul's words to the Corinthian Christians, in which he points out that the advantages are not all on one side.

Nowhere are marriage and parenthood stated to be the only pattern for a fulfilling life. There are many single people in the Bible whose state is accepted as perfectly normal. But today we have the problem of churches who have put a heavy emphasis on marriage to the detriment of friendship and the advantages of singleness – amidst a culture obsessed with sex. Society's pressures on women to be independent and self-sufficient serves only to highlight their underlying need of dependency and self-giving. Even with the knowledge of God's loving acceptance, many women still feel rejected and humiliated if they haven't had a proposal of marriage.

Paul Tournier rightly noted that "a spiritual miracle is absolutely necessary (to accept celibacy), without which the supposed acceptance is only chagrin and repression." So let's pray for miracles! We need to learn true acceptance because statistics decree that many will be single, at least for a large part of their lives. Only when we do learn true acceptance are we free to love in legitimate ways other than just within the marriage relationship.

Are you willing to pray for that miracle? You can only do so, I believe, if you are convinced that God's plan for you is not only good, but the best and, secondly, if the Cross is daily at the heart of your life.

 **Lord, deliver me from self-pity and from the pressures of the world around me. Grant me joy and excitement in realising all the potential you have placed in me.**

 *Do we all have a right to be married?*

*Are negative attitudes holding you back from becoming all that God intends you to be?*

**Psalm 91:1–16; Isaiah 40:10,11, 27–31; 54:4–14**

Single parents find themselves in the worst of all possible positions – the disadvantages of both marriage and singleness. Children, although providing company and purpose, tie up most of their time, energy and resources, making it hard to build friendships and join in activities. The complex emotions surrounding divorce, separation or grief over the death of a husband/wife have to be experienced without the time or emotional "space" to do so properly.

Practical help is usually a priority. There are many tasks a single parent may need help with – household chores, fixing something electrical or mechanical, cooking, shopping, financial...And, of course, there is the need for the occasional break from the children, whether they are babies, toddlers or older. It is best to offer specific help, for most of us single parents are reluctant to ask people who, we feel, have enough to cope with.

Single parents also need to know that they are still people in their own right rather than being seen *only* as people bringing up children. Opportunities to talk things through, invitations to dinner – both alone and with the children – and encouraging them to use their talents are all important. Psalm 68:4–6 is a lovely description of God and His care for those who are on their own. The home or family in verse 6 should be found in the local church, where imaginative help and sacrificial love towards the lonely should be much in evidence.

Surviving pressure is a big issue with a single parent. Sheer weariness is often the greatest enemy, along with having no one to share things with. Yet there is no reason why children of one parent families should end up damaged or deprived – not with a God who promises to be a father to the fatherless. But this promise needs to be fleshed out by Christian brothers and sisters who can share the load.

 **Father God, take my anxieties, my inadequacies, my weariness. May I know, hour by hour, that I can do everything necessary through Christ who strengthens me.**

*How can you cope with the temptation to panic or go under? (Look up Isa. 26:3,4; 2 Cor. 4:7–11).*

*Have you been experiencing God's strength being made perfect in your weakness?*

### DAY 6

**Job 23:1–7; Hebrews 10:32–11:1; James 1:2–4**

People who are single, bereaved or divorced struggle to recover from the hard knocks they have taken. They even wonder, at times, whether they will recover from their traumatic and tragic experiences. In so many situations it seems, at first, that God must have got it wrong. "Is he *really* in control? Surely this cannot be the right way...?" We question God's purpose for our lives.

Yet the Bible tells us that "in all things God works for the good of those who love him" – so that we will become like his Son (Rom. 8:28,29). "Lord, I can't handle this – it's destroying me!" cried one woman. "It won't destroy you," God told her, "it will strengthen you."

Of course God is concerned about our happiness, but not at any price. Nor is it His first aim for us. He loves us so much that He has the highest goal in mind for us: Christlikeness. In getting us there through the work of the Holy Spirit on our characters, He bears our anger, confusion, resentment, rejection and faithlessness – encouraging and comforting, knowing that when we fully see and understand we will have no complaints (Rom. 8:16–18).

I dragged my children to the top of Snowdon while we were on holiday – in thick mist. They told me I was mad. I told them it was a good test of endurance, walking more by faith and less by sight. I'd like to say the cloud lifted when we got there, but it didn't. That's life. But it will lift. And that's eternity.

 **Lord, help me to see that you are building on a scale I cannot begin to understand. Your purposes are good, eternal and will be established. I bow to your eternal wisdom.**

 *What is God wanting to build into your character?*

*"We will not know God's secret will until we've obeyed His revealed will,"* said R.T. Kendall. *How does this help when we don't understand?*

## DAY 7

**Romans 14:10–12; Psalm 22:1–31; Genesis 2:18**

At the heart of everything we have been looking at over the past few days is the fight against loneliness. There is, of course, an aloneness we must all accept whether we are married or single, surrounded by friends or not: alone before God. We need to learn to come by ourselves into His presence without fear or conditions and enjoy His love for us. We also need to accept ourselves enough to be able to enjoy our own company.

But God himself said it was not good for us to walk alone through life. We are not created to be self-sufficient, so we need to make the most of every relationship He provides. Marriage is not the only way of deepening our experience – family and friends are crucially important whether we are married or single. David reckoned his friendship with Jonathan was better than marriage! Such relationships are God-given to receive love, support and encouragement – and can be more enriching and rewarding than, perhaps, we've allowed them to be.

Sometimes we invite loneliness because we demand too much of others. If they are not just "right" we'd rather not bother. Such an attitude needs repenting of. Only God is perfect and only in Him will we ultimately find our answers. Usually, however, He will supply part of that answer through others – if we're ready to recognise and receive it with gratitude.

There are six principles which can help us through the complex problems of bereavement and loneliness: 1. Remember God's character. He loves and understands. 2. Know that in a fallen world suffering is inevitable. 3. Get hold of a perspective of eternity. 4. Look to God for security and direction. 5. Be willing to accept His plan and purpose. 6. Let Him minister to you through other relationships.

Lord, show me how to bring the truth of your Word into my situation, to know your love and healing power in a tangible way and be released from anything that holds back your purposes in my life.

---

## FOR GROUP DISCUSSION

● Can we be sure of life after death?

● What prevents us from coming alongside the bereaved and lonely and how can we deal with these hang-ups?

● Arthur was 79 when he died of a heart attack, having been married to Joan for 54 years without any children. Alex was 30 when he was killed in a car crash, leaving Sally and their two children, both under five. How are Joan's and Sally's situations (a) similar and (b) different?

● "Life can only really be understood when contrasted with death," said Elizabeth Casson. How is this true?

● What would you say in attempting to comfort someone grieving over the death of a husband or wife who, as far as it is known, never received Jesus as their Saviour?

● How important is it to warn people of the eternal consequences of ignoring Christ's offer of forgiveness?

● In what ways can the Church meet the needs of single people?

● Singles/single parents: are you fully accepted in your church and your particular gifts being used to the full?

---

### Suggested further reading

*Facing Bereavement* edited by Anne Warren (Highland)
*Dying: the Greatest Adventure of My Life* James Casson (CMF)
*Does God Care?* R.T. Kendall (Hodder & Stoughton)
*The Father Heart of God* Floyd McClung (Kingsway)
*Hereafter* David Winter (Mowbrays).

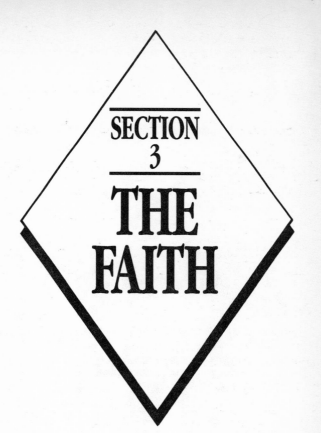

SECTION
3
THE
FAITH

# MAKING SURE

## Luis Palau

*Luis Palau is an internationally known evangelist who has been heard by millions of people around the globe through crusades, radio and television. Born in Buenos Aires, Argentina, he is married to Pat, whom he met at Bible school in the USA. The couple have four grown-up sons and live in Portland, Oregon, headquarters of the Luis Palau Evangelistic Association. Luis has led evangelistic crusades in Scotland, London and Wales.*

### DAY 1

**John 1:1–18**

I was in the middle of leading an evangelistic meeting in a large city church when I noticed a young man in a wheelchair. He was thin, pale and drawn. Although he could only have been in his thirties, he looked as if he was well on the way to death and eternity. Only afterwards did I find out that he had leukemia. Although he had long ago turned against God, he had let his Christian wife bring him to the meeting and, to her surprise, listened intently to the message. The Spirit of God was working in his heart and, when I gave the invitation to receive Christ, he was the first to come to the front.

Afterwards he said to me, "All my life I've been blasting God. When I contracted leukemia I became even more blasphemous. But tonight I realised that despite my antagonism, God loves me. I want eternal life. Do you think God will forgive me despite the awful things I've said about Him?" I opened my Bible and read him the Lord's promise that "Their sins and lawless acts I will remember no more (Heb. 10:17).

No matter what we have done in the past, each of us can receive forgiveness of sins and have assurance of eternal life. *Decision* is the key. We can't wash our hands like Pontius Pilate did after Jesus was betrayed, neither can we say, "I'll think about it sometime. "To all who received him, to those who believed on his name, he gave the right to become children of God" says verse 12 of our passage. To receive Jesus, we have to make a decision personally – and that decision is really quite simple. It's rather like a speaker saying, "As a memento of our meeting tonight, I want to give you my Bible. It has my name on it and some good notes inside. If you want it, come and get it." To have that gift, you have to get up and walk forward to receive it, say "Thank you" and it's yours.

"The wages of sin is death," says Romans 6:23, "but the gift of God is eternal life in Christ Jesus our Lord." That's why it's so important to say, in faith, "Thank you, Jesus. I receive you into my heart." The moment you do, your life changes forever.

 **Lord Jesus, thank you for the gift of eternal life. Forgive me for my sins and help me to be willing to acknowledge you as Lord of my life.**

 *What was your life like before you became a Christian?*

*How has your life changed since receiving the Lord Jesus Christ as your Saviour?*

 **Romans 10:8–15**

As C.S. Lewis once said, "No man is ready to live life on earth until he is ready for life in heaven." Committing your life to Jesus Christ is the most important decision you can ever make. Compared with that, all other decisions aren't that important. Contrary to popular myth, growing up in a Christian family doesn't automatically make someone a Christian, for God has no grandchildren. Each of us must come to personal faith in Christ.

I discovered that. Like so many others, I grew up attending Sunday school and church, hearing Bible stories and learning many Christian hymns and choruses. But I didn't know Jesus Christ. If someone asked me, I could stand up and say a prayer or quote a few Bible verses. But if something went wrong I cut loose with a string of dirty words. Deep down, I knew I wasn't right with God.

My parents had found forgiveness and joy by committing their lives to Christ thanks to the faithful witness of a Christian businessman from Britain. I deeply respected them and their faith, but I kept on fighting against owning up to my sins and receiving Christ myself until, one summer before I became a teenager, I was at a Christian camp in the mountains of Argentina. One night, the camp counsellor, Frank Chandler, and I were talking about what it means to become a Christian. He read verses 9 and 10 of today's passage to me: "If you confess with your mouth, 'Jesus is Lord,' and believe in your heart that God raised him from the dead, you will be saved..."

We talked about what this meant and he encouraged me to commit my life to Christ. I prayed, "Lord Jesus, I believe you were raised from the dead. I confess you with my lips. Give me eternal life. I want to be yours. Save me from hell. Amen." That night I could hardly sleep – I was so excited! I knew I was saved and a member of God's family for ever.

 **Dear Lord Jesus, thank you for the assurance I can have of eternity with you. I believe God raised you from the dead and I confess you as my Lord.**

 *How did you become a Christian?*

*Consider what it means to believe, to confess and to be saved.*

 **DAY 3**    **Acts 8:26 – 9:19**

There are such a variety of experiences at the point of conversion – just as there are so many varieties of people in the world. In Acts we see many different people confessing the Lord Jesus as Saviour. It took a crisis experience to bring some of them, like Saul the persecutor of the Church, to their knees. Others, like the Ethiopian eunuch, heard the Gospel and gladly trusted Christ. For most people, becoming a Christian is a memorable, though not necessarily dramatic, experience. Recalling when and where that decision was made enables us to counter-attack Satan when he assails us with doubts.

114

During times of doubt, I believe it's profitable to reaffirm our commitment to the Lord by telling him, "I *do* trust you. I *do* believe you. No matter what doubts and troubles come, I believe you're my Saviour." During our Christian pilgrimage, especially when we're younger, it can be helpful to reinforce our decision to trust Christ. My wife, Pat, and I can both recall telling the Lord as teenagers that we'd accepted Him previously but were now recommitting our lives to Him anyway. God knows what we are like and isn't surprised when we want to make sure we're saved (see Ps. 103:13,14).

Keith and Kevin, our twin eldest children, each prayed to receive Jesus when they were six years old – independently of the other. Equally independently, they were doing so every Sunday! We felt uneasy theologically about that, but God knows each heart, and that's what Keith and Kevin look back on now.

Some who are raised in Christian homes often commit their lives to Christ several times in different ways while they're growing up. Asked when they became a Christian, they might say, "The earliest decision I can remember is..." Others, like Billy Graham's wife, Ruth, can't remember a specific date when they received Jesus – but they can't remember a day when they didn't trust Him either. Whether or not you can recall an actual day when you trusted Jesus isn't essential. What *is* crucial is truly making that commitment. Then you can rest in the promises found in God's Word.

 **Dear Lord, I reaffirm the commitment of my life to you and your will. Help me to consistently remember your promises to me.**

 *Are you sure that your sins are forgiven and that you have eternal life?*

*What have you done during times of doubt?*

### John 10:27–29; 1 John 5:1–12

If you conducted an opinion poll in your neighbourhood and asked ten people to explain how a person can become a Christian, you would probably get ten different answers! I've met sincere people who say, "I was born a Christian" or "I've been a Christian all my life."

A few years ago I was meeting with some Scottish ministers when, during the lunch break, a man who had been in the ministry for 17 years said to me, "Luis, I don't know if I have eternal life." He then explained that two of my team members had visited him and his wife the night before and both happened to mention their assurance of eternal life. After they left, the minister asked his wife: "Do you have eternal life?" "I don't know," she replied. "Do you?" "You know that I don't," replied the minister. "What are we going to do?" She suggested that he talked with me. That afternoon he received eternal life and, soon afterwards, so did his wife.

Like that couple, you can *know* that you have eternal life. Jesus talked about those who had received Him by faith: "I give them eternal life, and they shall never perish; no one can snatch them out of my hand." Triple security – Christ's gift of eternal life, imperishable, unable to be snatched away from Jesus. What more could you want?

 **Lord Jesus, thank you for the promise of eternal life. Now I claim your promise of assurance.**

 *Do you know that you have eternal life?*

*What is your assurance of salvation based upon?*

### 1 John 1:5–10; Philippians 1:3–6

I was in London ready to start a major evangelistic campaign when a journalist came to interview me. "I've been up all night," he told me. "I'm glad you're here at the studio. You've got to save me!" I smiled. "Well," I replied, "I don't think I can save you, even if you have been up all night – but the Lord can."

Later I was on a Radio London programme when some-one phoned in to tell me, "I've been cynical about what hap-pens after you die, but you talk about eternal life as though it were real. Can we be sure?" So for the opening night of that mission, I talked about triple assurance, based on John 10:27 & 28. "My sheep listen to my voice," said Jesus. "I know them and they follow me." In other words, someone who trusts Jesus Christ believes Him and relies upon Him. A Christian also obeys the Lord, for opening our hearts to Jesus means not only believing in Him, but *following* Him.

"If I give my life to Christ I'm afraid that I won't follow Him, that I'll fail Him," people have told me. "I don't want to be a hypocrite – I already see too many people like that." But when you open your heart to Jesus Christ and ask Him to take control, the Holy Spirit will come to dwell in you, enabling you to both obey Him and faithfully witness in His name. And when we do slip and sin, we don't catch God off-guard. He has provided a way of restoration, as 1 John 1:9 tells us.

Until we see the Lord face to face, we won't be totally without sin, but God will complete the work He began in us and do good works *through* us. Let's take it to heart that we Christians are God's workmanship (Eph. 2:10).

 **Dear Lord, thank you for not giving up on me even when I'm at my worst. Help me to be aware of the sin in my life and cleanse me as I repent of it.**

 *Is your life characterised by obedience to the Lord?*

*In what ways has God already worked in your life?*

 **John 5:24–30; 10:22–30**

A sick and frail old lady attended an evangelis-tic rally where I was a guest speaker. When I invited people to go forward at the end of the service she was among those who publicly con-fessed Jesus as Saviour. "Why didn't someone tell me this before?" she cried. "Why did I have to wait until almost the end of my life?" Then she added, "I'm glad that at least I found out in my seventies." Six months later she went to be with the Lord – knowing she had eternal life because she had Jesus Christ in her heart. As verse 28 of our second passage assures us, Jesus gives those who follow Him eternal life and no one can snatch them away from Him.

Let's look a bit closer at this triple promise:

"I give them eternal life." Eternal life is a gift from God – in fact, eternal life is Jesus Christ himself. "God has given us eternal life, and this life is in his Son. He who has the Son has life; he who does not have the Son of God does not have life" (1 John 5:11,12). Next Jesus says "they shall never perish." We need never fear losing the life that God gives us, because Jesus laid down His life on the cross for *us* (Rom. 5:8) and for *our sins* (1 Cor. 15:3). The result is that "The blood of Jesus...purifies us from all sin" (1 John 1:7). There is no fear of eternity for the Christian, even though the process of dying can be disagreeable.

"No one can snatch them out of my hand." Even when Satan attacks us we're protected. During a BBC TV interview I was asked, "Do you really believe that Satan is an actual being who can influence people?" The Bible clearly answers Yes. Satan opposes all who follow Christ and tries to plant doubt in our minds. But the fact is that if we belong to God's Son, we are His for ever.

 **Lord Jesus, thank you for the assurance of eternal life with you. Help me to rely upon you completely when doubts and fears arise.**

 *Ponder on what Jesus did for you on the Cross and through His resurrection.*

*Are you looking forward to eternity? If not, why not?*

**DAY 7**

**2 Corinthians 5:6–21**

After the young John Wesley experienced "instantaneous conversion and immediate assurance" 250 years ago, the whole of Britain felt the impact over the next 50 years as he travelled some 250,000 miles across the length and width of the land, preaching 40,000 sermons. His message always had the same aim as he urged men, women, young people and children to make sure of their salvation. "If we never have any certainty of our being in a state of salvation," he said, "good reason it is that every moment should be spent not in joy but in fear and trembling; and then undoubtedly in this life we are of all men most miserable! God deliver us from such a fearful expectation as this!"

As Arthur Skevington Wood, his biographer, points out in *The Burning Heart*, "Wesley was firm in his conviction that those who are indeed children of God will not be left in doubt by the Holy Spirit." The Scriptures make this clear: "The Spirit himself testifies with our spirit that we are God's children. Now if we are God's children, then we are heirs — heirs with God and co-heirs with Christ, if indeed we share in his sufferings in order that we may share in his glory" (Rom. 8:16,17). And John adds that we know God lives in us "by the Spirit he gave us" (1 John 3:24).

But it's not enough to simply enjoy the Holy Spirit's assurance that we are saved and have eternal life, for He compels us to share the good news of Jesus Christ with others. May we, like John Wesley and so many others down the ages, be fervent and faithful witnesses to those we know or meet who have yet to hand their lives over to the Son of God.

 **Thank you, dear Lord, for the witness of the Holy Spirit that I am yours. Please help me to be an effective witness to your saving power.**

---

**FOR GROUP DISCUSSION**

- What is involved in becoming a Christian?

- What are the common myths about being a Christian?

- How would you respond to them?

- Do you find it easy to believe in Jesus' promise of eternal life or do you struggle with doubts?

- Are you more assured now of your salvation than you were before you began this week of studies?

- How does it matter whether we obey the Lord or fail Him in daily living?

---

# GROWING IN FAITH

## Stuart Pascall

*Stuart Pascall is an evangelist with Saltmine Trust. Living in Bournemouth with his wife, Margaret, and two children, he is Chairman of the Evangelical Alliance evangelism committee. Before joining Saltmine in 1988 he spent five years as Director of Evangelism and Youth Studies at Moorlands Bible College.*

## DAY 1

### Luke 8:22–25

Back at the turn of the century, a Methodist by the name of Jabez Bunting declared, "I'd rather go to sea in this little barque than perish on the sea shore." Sometimes the little barque (or small boat) of our Christian experience seems a very small dot on the vastness of the ocean of life. Perhaps it appears rather more like an out-of-control canoe being thrown about in white water rapids, at times threatened with being totally overwhelmed by the enormity of circumstances which seek to destroy our sometimes tenuous hold on God. Yet we are undoubtedly better off in our small boat than on the shore, for we do know that Someone is with us who is well versed in seamanship and has had experience of storm control!

As your faith develops, you will certainly encounter storms. But remember who is in control and think about the vastness of His ability. Reflect on His greatness.

Today's passage has all the ingredients for a shipping disaster: a small boat, fishermen – and a sudden and violent storm which whips the sea into a frenzy. The men would have been better off staying ashore – or would they? There is the little matter of a sleeping Saviour. Awakened by panic-stricken disciples, Jesus immediately calms the elements and then challenges the awestruck men: "Where is your faith?" That's the essential question if faith is to develop. The disciples were given the opportunity to reflect on their experience and learn a vital truth about Jesus:

"Even the winds and waves obey *Him*!" If they had stayed on the shore they would never have seen this.

As you seek to grow in faith, you will encounter sudden and sometimes severe storms. Don't be surprised nor hanker after the shore of the old days. It's in such times that you will see at firsthand the Master's power at work in your life. And when you feel a bit shaky remember that He's on constant storm patrol.

 **Lord, thank you that I am so small, because it helps me to see that I must trust you more for my faith to not just survive, but grow. Help me to deepen my roots in you, so that I may truly know you and your power to be made perfect in my weakness.**

 *How would you have reacted if you had been in the boat with the disciples?*

*Make an honest assessment on the state of your faith.*

 **Philippians 3:1–11**

A young mother stopped outside a post office and told her two sons to take some letters in, buy some stamps and post them. When they came out she asked them if everything was OK. "Yes, I posted the letters," said the four-year-old. "And I posted the stamps!" piped up his three-year-old brother.

To get to their destination, letters and stamps go together – just as in the Christian life growing in faith and knowledge of the Lord go hand in hand. At the end of the day it is not quality or quantity of our faith that's important, but the object of it. You can have a very strong faith on very thin ice and catch pneumonia to prove it! Or you can have very little faith on very thick ice and stay on it warm and secure.

The object of our faith is God in three persons – Father, Son and Holy Spirit. Knowing more and more about Him enables our faith to grow. The apostle Paul had an overwhelming desire to know Christ. As the Amplified Bible renders verse 10 of today's passage, "For my determined purpose is to know Him – that I may progressively become more deeply and intimately involved with Him, perceiving and recognising and understanding (the wonders of His person) more strongly and clearly."

Paul's growing understanding enabled him to cope with whatever trouble was thrown at him! Even in a Roman prison, where he wrote to the Christians at Philippi, his knowledge of Christ kept his faith firm. The more you know of Christ's character the more you will trust Him in every circumstance of life.

 **Dear Lord, it's not always easy being a Christian. Sometimes I get defeated by circumstances and feel I must be the world's biggest failure. But thank you that you have put the desire in me to know you. Help me to know you more and more, better and better.**

 *How keen are you to know Jesus more?*

*What have you learned about Christ recently?*

# DAY 3

**Isaiah 40:18–31**

When Lord Carnarvon, the famous archaeologist and Egyptologist, finally broke through into the tomb of King Tutankhamen, he gazed in awestruck silence at the glittering contents through his carefully excavated hole. Asked by those waiting impatiently behind him if he could see anything, he replied: "Yes, wonderful things." So it is with our study of the character of God. Our passage tells us so much about His greatness. The more we meditate on His attributes and discover "wonderful things," the more our reliance upon Him grows.

When I was a young Christian a number of years ago, I started reading a book called *Knowing God* by Jim Packer. As I did so, I began to discover great things about the character of God. "Knowing God," I recall Jim Packer saying, "involves listening to God's Word and receiving it as the Holy Spirit interprets it to oneself; noting God's character as His Word and works reveal it; doing what He commands; recognising, and rejoicing in, the love He has shown in approaching us, and drawing us, into this divine fellowship." These four pointers will help you on your way to a greater and more effective knowledge of God.

The reverse is also true, of course! The smaller our knowledge of God, the less sure our faith will be. Much of our wobbling and failure stems from a faulty perception of God. We feel threatened and weak – and suspect that the same is true of Him, as well as being powerless, unable and unwilling to help us! A right perspective of God will help us to stand strong and do great things.

 **Lord God, I really want to have a greater understanding of you. When I think of how great you are I am amazed! Thank you for your concern for me, that I'm not a collection of atoms, but a loved child.**

 *List the characteristics of God in today's passage. Which one excites you most? Why?*

*In a sentence of not more than 20 words, write a description of God.*

# DAY 4

### John 16:5–15

Residents of Blaenau Ffestiniog once demanded that the Welsh town should be fenced off, because it was being overrun by sheep, which had learned to escape by rolling over the cattle grids on their backs! As we develop our faith, we must gain a clear understanding of the power available to us to roll over any obstacles that get in our way. For Jesus makes it clear that we would not be left alone, but would have His Spirit living within us (John 14:17).

Jesus promised the disciples that when He went back to heaven He would send the Holy Spirit. The Spirit has all the characteristics of Jesus but, unlike Him, would be with His disciples all the time. He would work in the world (vv. 8–11) and also be in the disciples, leading them on a voyage of discovery (vs. 13). He is the divine messenger, bringing the power, ability, authority and character of Jesus right into your life. And, as the Man said, there's more! Note what Jesus said about the source of all His character (vs 15), the heart of the Father.

The Bible makes it clear that the Holy Spirit is an integral part of our journey of faith. As He fills the "barque" we discover an ability and authority that is far beyond human level, for it flows from the heart of God. It is no wonder that we can roll over the obstacles, for we discover that His power is made perfect in weakness (2 Cor. 12:9).

 **Lord Jesus, thank you for sending the Holy Spirit to dwell in me. Help me to allow the Spirit to develop a character that is more like you.**

 *What difference did the coming of the Holy Spirit make to the disciples?*

*In what ways should the indwelling of the Holy Spirit in us show?*

## DAY 5

**Ephesians 6:10–18**

"Three hundred dozen eggs were stolen from a farm at Moorby. Poachers are suspected!" reported the *Grimsby Evening Telegraph*. One of the biggest poachers of our faith is the devil, who has a vested interest in hindering our developing knowledge of God. Satan is bent on destroying our reliance upon Him. Among the weapons in his armoury are two particularly destructive ones – doubt and uncertainty.

Way back, at the start of God's relationship with Adam and Eve, His character was called into question. "Did God really say...?" (Gen. 3:11). "You will not surely die" (Gen. 3:4). The devil's dealings with Eve clearly shows his strategy of poaching trust, for in a few words he destroyed her ability to trust God, making her doubt the source of her life and power. So she wandered into confusion and, eventually, sin. We when we lose our grip of God's reliability and trustworthiness we become confused and rebellious.

The apostle Paul warned the Corinthian Christians of Satan's aim to outwit, reminding them not to be ignorant of the enemy's schemes (2 Cor. 2:11). Paul wrote to the believers in Ephesus to tell them that there is an unrelenting attack going on (vs. 10 of today's passage). It appears in a variety of ways – physical onslaught, moral temptation, social pressures and spiritual darkness. That's why an essential armour must be worn (vv. 13–17). With this on we will have an essential awareness of the battle and when the attack is finished you will still be standing up.

My wife's family have a dog which will, when commanded, lie down and play dead. There are too many Christians who lie down and play dead to avoid unwelcome attention. Don't be one of those. We are born to battle – and the only way to overcome is to keep on going forward, trusting in God's generous provision. Then we will be able to resist the one bent on poaching our faith through doubt and uncertainly. Don't listen to him – listen to God!

 **Lord, I know there's a battle raging and that, as I keep on going forward with you, I face attack in all sorts of ways, both felt and unseen. Thank you for your armour, which is the complete answer to the devil's schemes.**

 *What kind of spiritual attacks have you faced recently?*

*How can you ensure that you are fully equipped for battle each day?*

## DAY 6

**Genesis 12:1–8**

"Thirty-eight years on the same spot!" proclaimed a sign proudly put up by a well-established firm of laundry and dry cleaners. The journey we make in our "small barque" of Christian experience means that we can never remain on the same spot. Faith must develop and grow as time goes by. We began our journey *by faith* and are to continue it in the same way. We are aided, encouraged and cheered on by the whole of the Godhead.

Abraham began his journey by faith. God spoke to him and made promises, so Abraham, although getting on in years, gave up his comfortable lifestyle and set off on a long trek, together with all relations, friends and, more especially, with God. As Hudson Taylor, the pioneer missionary to China, put it: "All God's saints have been weak men who did great things for God, because they reckoned on God being with them."

125

That's why Abraham got going – he reckoned God was with him. I've a sneaking suspicion that he didn't know much about God when he set out (probably a bit like you and me), but he responded to what he had discovered. It's interesting to note that twice in this passage "he built an altar". He responded by recognition, submission and worship. As we sense God speaking to us, we need to worship. As we respond to Him, we discover the flow of His love, which takes us on to the next stage of the journey.

It's in hearing and responding that we find ourselves moving on, sometimes rapidly, sometimes imperceptibly – but encouraged in the knowledge that the evidence of real life is growth.

 **Lord, Abraham must have been a remarkable character to go off on that long journey, but I really do want to have that sort of relationship with you that will enable me to respond to your voice. Speak to me today and give me the ability to trust you.**

 *Have you heard God speaking to you recently? How have you responded?*

*How healthy is your worship life?*

**DAY 7**

**Psalm 27:1–14**

We have thought and studied, over the past few days, about the journey that the "little barque" of our Christian faith has to make across the ocean of life. While we may feel threatened by the things that happen around us, as well as to us, we have a Fellow Traveller who makes us invincible. He's a companion whose power is unlimited, whose ability is unquestioned and whose presence is undeniable. He is God!

In our relationship with Him, it is essential that our ability to trust Him is developed. This happens as we see who He really is and what He is able to do.

The psalm we are studying tells of a man's confidence in God's ability to protect him when evil men attack and even when a whole army is against him (vv. 2 & 3). His desire is to spend more time with God (vv. 4–6), so that he can learn how to live aright (v. 11). No matter what happens, God's goodness will be made known to him (v. 13), so no wonder he encourages us to wait for the Lord (v. 14).

You can be sure that your faith has grown in the past week as you've worked through these studies, if for no other reason than you've stopped to think about the God who promised to be with you always. Trust Him and His ability – not your own strength!

 **Dear Lord, thank you that I can totally trust you day by day. Help me to continue to grow in the knowledge of you and reflect you in the needy world through which I journey with you.**

---
### FOR GROUP DISCUSSION
---

● What have you learned most about growing in faith in the past week?

● Share about storms you've encountered recently – and what the Lord Jesus did in those difficult circumstances.

● Why does faith grow in adversity?

● How do you define faith?

● What area of your life do you feel you need help in to enable you to grow?

● What does it mean to be filled with the Holy Spirit?

● Abraham heard God speak. How does God speak to us today?

● In what ways can we worship God?

● A friend became a Christian yesterday. How would you encourage him/her to grow in faith?

# WORDS, WORKS AND WONDERS

## Roger Forster

*Roger Forster was converted to Christ at Cambridge University. He is the founder and leader of Ichthus Christian Fellowship in inner London, which comprises a church fellowship, ministry team and training programme. He has evangelised and taught the Scriptures in many parts of the world and has run a home for people with social problems. The author of four books, including* God's Strategy in Human History, *he is married to Faith, who is also actively involved in ministry. They have three children.*

**Romans 5:17–20; Acts 10:34–44**

Too often Christians divide over issues which need to be held in harmony, like the subject we have begun to tackle today – putting our faith into action. Its three parts should really be kept together. One group of believers say we must evangelise by words, preaching, witnessing with our mouths, debating and teaching and not bother about good works or signs and wonders. The world, they explain, will go from bad to worse, so why try to relieve social problems? They also believe that, as signs and wonders come from God, we can't do anything about them.

Another group, whom we can call evangelical social activists, say that we all talk too much. Men and women, they assert, are waiting to see our good works and then they will turn to God – Jesus said as much in the Sermon on the Mount. We evangelise by our Christ-like action and, since the day of miracles has passed, signs and wonders come from false prophets, who will deceive people.

Other Christians put little confidence in preaching. We must, in their view, demonstrate good news that God is with us by signs and wonders. Jesus needed signs and wonders,

128

declaring that even Sodom would have repented if it had been ministered to in such a way (Matt. 11:23). We hear too many words but see too little evidence of God's power. The Word of God (they rightly assert) must be demonstrated.

Paul, however, keeps all three aspects together and calls them, collectively, evangelism. The apostle ministered in the power of the Spirit of God. Jesus himself preached peace, did good things and healed through the anointing of the Holy Spirit. All three strands are found in today's passages. True evangelism is still to invade our society with Holy Spirit words, works and wonders. Unless we use all three instruments of evangelism in the power of the Spirit, preaching is merely intellectual, good works empty humanism and signs and wonders could deceive ourselves and others (2 Thess. 2:9,10).

**Lord Jesus, please give me boldness to speak, love to act and faith to see signs and wonders, so that I might be used more in evangelism by you.**

*Is your evangelism balanced like Paul's? If not, what can you do to rectify it?*

*In the light of today's study, how can you discern whether signs and wonders are of God or the enemy?*

**John 9:1–8**

One of the ways we are meant to serve society in the name of Jesus is by revealing the works of God. In our fellowship is an ex-Muslim family who turned to Christ soon after two of our members helped them in their home when their baby was ill. They also offered to pray for the baby, the offer was accepted and the child was healed. Through a word of knowledge, one of our workers visited a lonely lady. That Sunday she came to the meeting, was saved and healed there and then! We often offer to pray for sick people as we go from door to door during a street meeting. Loneliness, fear and pain are always a challenge for Christians to reach out their hands and change things.

Too often we are like the disciples in today's reading.

When confronted with suffering we are content with a theological answer rather than doing something about it. "Who sinned, Lord, that this man was born blind?" Imagine what this man must have felt, being discussed as a theological problem instead of receiving compassion.

Unfortunately, most translations make Jesus give a strange caricature of God in His answer. It seems, indeed, that God made the man blind to heal him and then get glory for Himself. But the Father of our Lord Jesus isn't like that. We don't have to punctuate the sentence in that way. The answer to the disciples' question should read: "Neither this man sinned nor his parents." (Full stop). *New sentence:* "But that the works of God should be made manifest in him we must work the works of Him that sent me while it is still day." (This construction occurs in other places in the Greek text of John's gospel, such as 1:31; 14:31; 15:25).

Wherever we find suffering in our society, we must reach out hands to work with Jesus to see things change — such as alcoholism, drug addiction, unmarried mothers, AIDS, pregnancy counselling to save unborn babies. The works of God bring life, sight and healing to society's victims.

 **Dear Father, there is so much need in the world. Please direct me to where I am to serve with Jesus.**

 *Are you content with mere theological answers or do you want to get involved?*

*What is an area of human suffering in which my church can get involved?*

 **Hebrews 11:17–19; James 2:20–24; Genesis 22:1–4**

To be pleasing to God, our works must be faith-motivated, for it is faith which gives room for God's activity by His Spirit. Often the teachings of Paul and James about faith and works are set over against each other as though they are contradictory. But we are meant to see that Paul speaks about works of the *law* done to justify ourselves. Rather, we need faith to let God in and justify us. James speaks of *works* of faith, which

WORDS, WORKS AND WONDERS

show that God has moved in and goes beyond anything we could accomplish through our activities.

If we think we can accomplish some good works or project ourselves with our own abilities, we don't need faith. If, on the other hand, it is utterly impossible without God, it will have to be a faith work. It's that kind of work which real believers are called upon to perform. As they bring such works to completion, they show they have real faith.

Abraham let God in by faith as he offered up Isaac. He knew he couldn't do it without God and couldn't receive him back unless God raised up Isaac again. Abraham's act was fruit from the real tree of faith within him. It was so powerful that it served all mankind, for the offering of Isaac on Mount Moriah revealed Calvary love ahead of time at the very place where Jesus would be crucified 2,000 years later.

When we do a good work in faith and obedience to God, we minister more than just the little bit we do. For we give God the opportunity to reveal His love supernaturally in our act of faith. More is accomplished by Him than is ever done by us. When we dried out Grandmother after her basement flat had been flooded, her granddaughter (a mother of about 35), banged on my door saying, "How can I become a Christian?" She saw more than a good work – she saw Jesus.

 **Lord Jesus, help me to believe in all I do so that you have ground to work from in my life.**

 *In the light of this study, what does the parable of the mustard seed mean? (Matt. 13:31, 32)*

*Do you try to evangelise out of duty or are you expecting God to step in by faith?*

 **Matthew 5:1–16; Genesis 22:7, 8**

The Matthew passage, from the Sermon on the Mount, contains the first statement about the new people of God, the Church, which is being called into being by Jesus. In the first ten verses, Jesus speaks of people in the third person – "Blessed

131

are *they*." But he changes to the second person in verse 11 – "Blessed are *you*" – and shows that the basis of this new society is found in the close relationships His disciples have with Himself. They are persecuted falsely for "my sake." This persecution identifies them with those of the past who had a "prophetic" calling (v. 12). They, too, will act as salt and light in society around them. Their prophetic, salty, lighting works will show men that God the Father is with them and evoke His praise.

The Church is the latter day prophetic instrument, but Abraham is the first man in Scripture to be called a prophet (Gen. 20:7). We and Abraham are in the same train! Abraham's life was a prophetic statement yet he only preached one brief sermon: "My son, God will provide Himself a lamb" (Gen. 22:8). This cleared the ground for the crucifixion of Jesus in the same place 2,000 years later. "God was in Christ reconciling the world to Himself" (2 Cor. 5:19).

As the Church prophesies by life and lip, we call mankind to see not only our good works, but the fact that the Father works with us. The Church's calling in words, works and wonders is *individually* as grains of salt to preserve and *corporately,* like a city, to enlighten the world with beams of light. When we do our marches for Jesus, we are acting prophetically together. Our church life should demonstrate a better way of sharing and caring. Any service to the community, from challenging the local council to running rescue shops for the destitute, reflect the calling of the Church to be salt and light.

 Father God, forgive me that I haven't always lived with my brothers and sisters as a unified city. Please show me if there is anyone I need to get right with or who needs my love.

 *What does it mean for you to be salt?*

*What things are wrong in your church that prevent members from speaking and acting prophetically?*

**Isaiah 58:1–14; Hosea 6:6**

The Old Testament contains many passages which emphasise the need for social justice. Often the prophets attacked religion for being a substitute for true obedience to God, which involved living righteously and being compassionate to one's neighbours. Jesus Himself twice quotes Hosea 6:6 (Matt. 9:13; 12:7).

Our first passage is one of the most forthright condemnations of hypocritical religion. The issues it raises are just as applicable to us now. Isaiah is told to spell out the people's sins because they couldn't see them. Religious practices can blind us to our sin. Despite attending meetings, their fasting and religious posturings were unacceptable to God.

True fasting involves taking action over the abuse of and misuse of people (v. 6). All four things Isaiah lists misuse the people through such things as under-paying for work, exploiting minority groups and the disadvantaged and taxing the poor. God is utterly opposed to such practices – and (v.7) expects us to take action by feeding the hungry (Mark 6:34–44; 8:1–9), providing a home for the poor homeless (Luke 12:12–14), clothing the naked (Matt. 25:43) and welcoming, rather than rejecting, such people (Luke 16:14–31).

Obedient adjustments in these areas will produce real spiritual flow in our lives and churches. We shall be like a watered garden – and we shall fulfil our calling to be a city set on a hill.

 **Lord, save me from religion and make me Christ-like in my relationships with those around me, that I might bring them justice, peace and joy.**

 *Do any of the indictments of Isaiah 58:6 convict you as either an employer or employee?*

*What steps can you and your church take to fulfil the things listed in verse 7?*

**Luke 14:12–24**

These two stories are linked together in Jesus' teaching and show us the right response to His invitation of grace. In the latter, we were the poor, lame, maimed and blind who had nothing to give back but, thanks to His free offer of salvation, we shall fill His house and eat His supper. So when we open our house and have a party, we are to invite those who can't repay us.

Rick Thomas's Bible study group felt God speak to them about the first story. So they took their Christmas dinner on to the rubbish tip in Juarez, where many people scratched a living. They had enough food for 150, but as they shared it they miraculously fed 300 — and left the people with even more food in their hands! This led to a supernatural transformation of the area and dedicated social concern. Exploiters have been removed or converted, jobs created and houses built, the sick healed and the dead raised to life. A farm and co-operative provide jobs and food. It's one of the most exciting Holy Spirit renewals of society this century.

More modestly in London, we have held parties for the elderly, cripples and the lonely, especially at Christmas. All those who come to these Jesus Action suppers are unable to pay. After one such evening of eating, entertainment, chat and the sharing of God's love, one lady said to me, "If God is like that, I want more of Him."

We can't lose out in giving out, says Jesus. At the resurrection of the saints, we will be rewarded by seeing many who couldn't repay us at God's supper. We at Ichthus often remind ourselves that the inner city has so much bad news that it needs celebration and party evangelism to show the Gospel to be *good* news.

 **Thank you, Lord Jesus, that you are coming again and we shall all enjoy the marriage supper of the Lamb. Please show me how to get ready for this.**

 *Do you convey Christianity as a party or a purgatory?*

*What sort of people in your area could do with a good party?*

**Galatians 5:6,13,14; Luke 10:25—37**

The story of the Good Samaritan, in a sense, sums up all the studies in this section. It is love which is the ultimate, effective motivator for world evangelism and change in society. But often the point of the story is missed. Its aim is not simply to get us to "Go and do likewise," for we must love God first. Then there will be enough love to overflow from the source of all love to my neighbour as well.

God is lovable because He is like Jesus. As I commit myself to Him and keep coming to Him, I'm filled with love and can go and do likewise.

In love we have prayed for protection of people in London. Twelve hundred prayed publicly that a notorious killer terrorising the area would quickly be arrested and that he wouldn't commit any more murders. Thirty-six hours later he was caught. We have worshipped in areas torn by racial riots and in Jesus' name raised our voices about local public issues — council problems, misuse of public money and other injustices. We have sought to do this without hate or fear, but with love and concern, so that our neighbours might be blessed and cared for on the Jericho roads of our lives.

All discrimination on the basis of race, class and sex (Gal. 3:28), must give way to the new mankind in Jesus. We are here to serve in compassion across all barriers, just as the Samaritan did, and to bring the benefits of the Kingdom of God to all men.

 **Show me, Lord, where I am religiously, denomination-ally, racially, nationally, economically, socially and sexually discriminatory.**

---

## FOR GROUP DISCUSSION

- Why is it that some Christians are afraid that serving society will hinder people from coming to Christ?

- What can be done to avoid social action being merely humanistic?

- If we refer to social action or signs and wonders as evangelism, will it mean that we are only using these things to get people saved? Does it matter?

- Is it more important to pray for your MPs and local councillors or to vote for them?

- How can we bring more of the Kingdom of God into our society? Make a list of ways, objectives, projects and so on.

- Spend five minutes in silent prayer in your house/Bible study group, asking God to show you where there is injustice, discrimination or unfairness to workmates, employees, employers, neighbours or families.

---

### Suggested further reading

*Rich Christians in an Age of Hunger* Ron Sider (Hodder & Stoughton)
*Bias to the Poor* David Sheppard (Hodder & Stoughton)
*The Call for Conversion* Jim Wallis (Lion).

# WORKING IT OUT

## Philip Herbert

*Philip Herbert is managing director of Jasper Herbert Ltd., a London-based fashion company. For the last nine years he has led a Bible study group for men at his church in Surrey and, on a national level, is involved with Christian Viewpoint for Men, a ministry which teaches how to reach men for Christ.*

**DAY 1**

**Genesis 1:26–28; 2:4–20**

"I love work. I could look at it for hours!" Perhaps this brings a wry smile to your face. Work has a very bad press, being portrayed as something we are made to do to survive, something we were made to do as children, perhaps as punishment. But it wasn't always so. God is introduced to us on the first page of the Bible as a God at work.

Jesus speaks about Him being like that (John 5:17). It is not surprising to see that, in making man and woman in His likeness, He gives them work to do – work both for their hands (agriculture, v.15; mining, v.12) and work for their heads (classification, v.20).

It is important to realise that work is a gift from a loving Father to His children – work that has to be done in partnership with the Father. Adam was needed to work the ground, but God watered it. Sin spoiled this special working relationship (3:8), but today the Lord Jesus lovingly invites us to enter into partnership with Him (Matt. 11:28,29).

In this partnership we find a total new approach to work. Also we find job satisfaction (Eccl. 3:13), that we can serve the community (Eph. 4:28) and we know that we bring glory to God in doing even a mundane job (Ex. 37:1, for instance).

 Thank you, Lord, for the gift of work and for the working relationship I have with you. Whatever I put my hand to today, may I do it with all my might.

*Before sin entered the world, men and women were busy at work in partnership with God. Does this revise your view of heaven?*

*How do you view your work today in terms of satisfaction, service and God's glory?*

### Nehemiah 1:1–2:9

Biographies of famous and successful people can inspire us. The Bible contains many biographies and some are especially of interest to those who aspire to positions of responsibility — Joseph, David and Daniel, for instance. Nehemiah is another, and his story forms the basis for the rest of these studies. I recommend reading the whole book of Nehemiah in a paraphrase such as the Living Bible to help catch the excitement of the narrative.

As "cupbearer", Nehemiah had a big job. In charge of the royal cellars, he would also choose the wines and taste them before handing them to the king. So he had constant access to the man at the top and had his confidence. Nehemiah was tough and determined, but he was also genuinely spiritual. His prayer (1:5–11), shows an understanding of God, an awareness of sin and a working knowledge of the Scriptures. He was, nonetheless, businesslike, even with God, and prayed specifically — "Give...success today...by...this man" (1:11).

Nehemiah so desperately wanted to talk to the king about Jerusalem that it affected his appetite, but he was sensitive enough to wait four long months for the right moment. Then, when it came, fear set in. But, being a man of prayer, he instinctively shot up a prayer before answering his employer.

The timing was the only surprise, for he knew precisely what he wanted to ask the king. His presentation of the problem shows sensitivity, courtesy, decisiveness and careful preparation. And yet, when he pulled it off, he was convinced it was God's doing (2:8).

**Help me, Lord, to serve my earthly boss with conviction, whether it will be appreciated or not, knowing that you see it as heart service to you.**

*Although Nehemiah was not exactly witnessing to his boss, what can we learn from his example of waiting for the right moment?*

*Do you find it hard to accept that the man who could pray the prayer in 1:5–11 was an expert in wines and earned his living by them? Pray today for any Christians you know of who are in unlikely occupations.*

**Nehemiah 2:10–20**

Nehemiah set himself the task of rebuilding the walls of Jerusalem. He left a good job at the centre of things where he was highly thought of by the king. The new job involved directing a run-down concern in which the people were demoralised and the competitors were strong and ruthless. Having made sure he had the backing of the king and the resources to do the work, he faced the real challenge of motivating the people.

What tests you most at work? Isn't it people? Whether bosses, colleagues or employees, people at work are often problems. Nehemiah knew this only too well – his life depended on the people's co-operation. The state of the city was almost certainly the result of malice on the part of neighbouring "colleagues" (see Ezra 4:6-23). Office politics held no surprises for Nehemiah.

To justify the king's support, he had to get the people motivated – people who until then, were content to just hang around in such a hopeless place. But again Nehemiah prepared himself thoroughly, willingly working unsociable hours (v.10). His words to the "management team" were chosen carefully. He gave an analysis of the situation, showing how his solution would benefit the workforce – "we will no longer be in disgrace" (v.17). He made them think they could succeed (v.18) and fired them up to decide to start work right away. It was their decision.

Doing everything right did not prevent the scorn and threats from the opposition, however. But Nehemiah had committed himself to trust God and, therefore, a polite but unequivocal response was quite sufficient.

Lord, help me to work out what it means for me today to go the extra mile, particularly as far as work is concerned.

 *How would your work improve by more planning and preparation the night before?*

*Who causes you problems at work? Pray for them and consider what you can do today to develop a better working relationship with them.*

**Nehemiah 3:1–5; 4:1–23**

Nehemiah was a success. He enjoyed the king's favour. He had adequate resources to rebuild the city, and the people were behind him. He was also a man whom God was blessing. What more could he have? Problems!

*Non co-operation.* Priests (3:1), perfumers (3:8) and even the mayor's daughters (3:12) were willing to do the manual work under supervision, but not the nobles of Tekoa (3:5). Was it the nature of the work they despised? Work much later dignified by Jesus, "the carpenter's son"? Nehemiah made sure they could see the benefit to themselves by letting them build near their own homes.

*Opposition.* Nehemiah was only rebuilding a small city, yet he became the target of intense hatred by his colleagues (fellow governors, 4:7). It is often the experience of the Christian who works conscientiously, for the world hates Christ's followers (John 15:19, 20). The tactics don't change – ridicule (4:1), ganging up (4:2) and a sneering reference to one's faith (4:3). The only answer is no answer – and plenty of prayer.

*Low morale* (4:10–14). Eventually the workers became discouraged by the size of the task, the strength of the opposition and the risk to family and friends. Keeping people motivated means understanding their needs and responding promptly and positively. A private pep talk to his management team was how Nehemiah faced this problem. Reassured, they would reassure others.

The demands and stress of protection were additional burdens to people already exhausted (4:10). Nehemiah made the same sacrifices (4:23) and proved himself to be a true leader, turning even the crises into success – a success he attributed entirely to God (4:15).

 **Help me, Lord, to see problems today as your means of developing a Christ-like character and, as such, to count them a joy.**

 *In what ways will the work you plan to do today benefit the community at large?*

*Are you experiencing a crisis at work right now? Pray that the Lord will show you how to turn it to advantage.*

## DAY 5

**Nehemiah 5:1–19**

Some years ago a friend of mine was sent by his firm on his first trip to the USA. When he came back to Britain he submitted his expenses claim – but his boss returned it. He had been "too honest" and would incriminate his colleagues who loaded theirs, so he was asked to increase it. To break with recognised practice when you are a new boy requires courage. Nehemiah might have been excused for ignoring the situation that had been tolerated by his predecessors, for he only took the job to rebuild the wall. But people are more important than projects, so he took their complaints seriously (v.7).

He "pondered" first, which, in his case, would almost certainly mean praying. He knew the Scriptures and worked out the principles involved. Those made poor by misfortune must, he decided, have the opportunity of becoming self-supporting again and deserved help from their neighbours. Convinced of this himself, he was able to persuade the officials to do the right thing.

Not only was Nehemiah a man of prayer with a practical understanding of the Scriptures, he also had principles and self-restraint. As governor, he was entitled to perks – and some justifiable ones at that. But he refused them "out of reverence for God" and because it meant a heavy demand on the people (v.15). In other words, he went without because he loved God and loved his neighbour.

This would almost certainly have upset the former governors and their servants, with whom he probably had to work. It is a familiar problem today to many Christians who have to work under the same principles. Such integrity demonstrated how Nehemiah was able to win over the officials when he took the bull by the horns and dealt with a problem he had inherited.

 **May my life at work today be as salt in its effect and light in its example through Jesus Christ our Lord.**

 *Verse 19 suggests that, having taken a decision on principle, Nehemiah had moments of self-doubt about the outcome. This experience is not uncommon to Christians at work. Why do you think God allows it? (Ps. 77:2a).*

*How does loving God and your neighbour affect your lifestyle at work?*

**DAY 6**

**Nehemiah 6:1–14**

A Christian managing director was concerned about the performance of his directors – Christians, too. When it was necessary to work extra hours, there was invariably a meeting at church which had to come first. That morning, three of them arrived late for the board meeting. So the boss decided to announce a prayer meeting to start 15 minutes before the next meeting. Everyone was punctual for that.

So meetings matter more than work for some Christians. Not for Nehemiah. His fellow governors suggested a meeting on the plain of Ono (v.2) "Ono?" responded Nehemiah. "Oh, no!" To have accepted would have meant a day's travelling, wasting valuable time at the meeting and a day getting back to the city. To have attended would have interfered with the work God had given him. An attempt to get him to agree to a more "spiritual" meeting was attempted, but again Nehemiah refused to go. He saw the reason behind the invitation and, in any case, he would not enter the part of the temple reserved for priests only.

Today it seems that many lay people – successful businessmen particularly – could learn from Nehemiah's humility. Too often they assume too much influence in the life and ministry of their local church solely because of their success in making money.

Nehemiah was convinced of the importance of his work and would not be easily put off. He listened to those who claimed they had a word from the Lord, tested it and rejected it as false. Knowing when to say "No" is essential.

 **Strengthen my hands to work with all my might, Lord, strengthen my mind to be committed to my calling, strengthen my will to be firm to finish the work you have given me.**

 *If you are asked to attend a meeting which would clash with a work commitment, would you (a) go to it; (b) say "No" or (c) pray about it? If your answer is (c), compare it with Nehemiah's prayer (v.9). Was it a prayer for guidance?*

*Can you detect any traces of superiority in your attitude to apparently less successful members in your church?*

**DAY 7**

**Nehemiah 6:15–7:3; 12:27–43**

It's early morning and outside there are already people at work. Pilots are high up, their planes almost out of sight. Each is leaving a contrail in the sky which, when touched by the rising sun, becomes brilliant and golden. They are just doing a job, obeying orders. They do not realise the good effect it has on me just now. Perhaps you are doing this study before starting another routine day (go to work, come home, go to bed, go to work...). But it's not like that when you belong to Christ. Work is a partnership with Him and, although it is not always apparent to you, everything you do for Him today will be touched with His glory.

We have seen how, again and again, Nehemiah talked to God at work. He knew Him well because he studied the Scriptures and was obedient to them. Nehemiah understood people and worked to get them a fair deal, but he did not stop there. He was an achiever, self-disciplined, worked out his priorities, set goals, faced up to problems and got results.

Then he called a celebration – a Christian in-word these days, but this was a celebration of work! When the work began, the first of the builders dedicated his labours to God (3:1). Now it was finished, they all gave thanks to Him (12:40).

Centuries ago a kitchen servant learned this secret and called it the "practice of the presence of God". Before starting each task, offer it to Him. Then, when it is finished, thank Him and offer it again. If you persevere, you will develop a good working relationship with God – and others will be blessed by it.

 Thank you, Lord, for those like Nehemiah who taught by their lives that the joy of the Lord is their strength. Help me today to be both joyful and strong in the work you have given me to do.

---

### FOR GROUP DISCUSSION

● Discuss experiences, positive and negative, of witnessing to colleagues and workmates, and draw out practical guidelines.

● Consider what motivates the people with whom you work. How should a Christian manager attempt to motivate his or her staff?

● Share experiences when you have not been sure of what was the right thing to do as a Christian at work. What effects have these times had on your relationship with the Lord?

● In what ways should you exercise self-restraint in the benefits you gain from your job?

● How can your minister/pastor better understand the demands that work makes on church members? Would it help if members of your group invited him to spend a day with them at their work?

● Is it possible to arrange vital meetings at times more suitable to working schedules – perhaps at breakfast time?

# WHAT ABOUT PROSPERITY?

## Trevor Partridge

*Trevor J. Partridge is a CWR Executive Director and responsible for the development of Waverley Abbey House, near Farnham, as a Christian Training Centre. He studied theology in America and trained as a counsellor. Married to Debbie, he has been involved in counselling and in developing a Christian counselling programme in the UK as well as teaching in seminars, conferences and churches in various parts of the world.*

**Joshua 1:1–9**

The days were crucial for Israel. Their trusted leader had died before he had achieved his ambition of bringing them into Canaan – the promised land. A new leader, Joshua, had been appointed. As he gazed across the Jordan river at the land of their dreams, I suspect he was wondering whether he would succeed where the great Moses had failed. Then God spoke to him, giving him encouragement and the keys to success and prosperity:

1. He was to be obedient to God's Word.
2. He was to speak God's Word.
3. He was to meditate on God's Word day and night.
4. He was to do what was written in it.

The principles for a successful and prosperous life are contained in the Scriptures. *Success* is almost a dirty word to many Christians. To them it is tainted with worldliness and selfish ambition, which is understandable living in a society where success is based on greed, acquisitiveness, extravagance and materialistic excess.

Weakness, unworthiness and failure are seen as more acceptable for Christians. So there has arisen this *worm* theology which says we are worthless and hopeless and must grovel before God for the rest of our lives. Yet God clearly promised Joshua success and prosperity – if he obeyed His conditions. Because Joshua did so (see his epitaph in Josh. 31:31), he prospered. And God promises the same for us (Eph. 1:18). He has not called us to impoverishment and failure, but wants us to prosper and be healthy (3 John 2).

 **Lord, help me, like Joshua, to know your Word and meditate upon it continually, so that I may know success in fulfilling your purposes.**

 *Find several instances in the book of Joshua where the four aspects of God's Word are seen in his life.*

*How are they at work in your life?*

**Luke 9:23–27**

Success is achieving your full potential in God. Our heavenly Father created you for a definite purpose. He has a plan for your life that is just perfect for you. He wants your life to count for Him, for you to make a significant impact where you live and work. God did not create you for failure, but that you might achieve your maximum potential in Him by becoming the person He always wanted you to be. As the apostle Paul put it, God decided from the very beginning that we should be "conformed to the likeness of His Son" (Rom. 8:29).

Jesus Christ is the most important person who ever lived, but so many people see Him as a failure because He died on a cross. God, however, was working His purposes out in His Son's suffering and death, so that seeming failure became the greatest success story of all – triumph and victory over sin, death and Satan.

This is all anathema to a world plunging deeper and deeper into materialistic *success*. The Cross means death to personal ambition, selfishness, covetousness, greed and the lust for power. The Cross is *not*, as some believe, the gateway and guarantee to health, wealth and boundless materialistic prosperity. God does not bring us to the Cross so that we can act like spoilt children, demanding what we want when we want. We cannot expect Him to act like a indulgent grandfather, handing out His riches at our whims and dictates.

If parents gave a child everything he or she wanted every time they demanded it, the youngster would soon become very self-centred. The Cross is the place where we surrender self-interest and selfish ambition, opening our hearts, as children of God, to His perfect purposes for our lives. His plan for us is success, not failure (Jer. 29:11).

 **Lord, I come afresh to the Cross, recognising that my life can only be successful and worthwhile as I surrender my personal ambition and self-interest to you.**

 *What is the truth that Paul brings out in Galatians 2:20?*

*What does Paul mean by* conformed *in Romans 12:2?*

## DAY 3

**1 Timothy 6:1-12**

We live in an age of rampant materialism. Our consumer, *loadsamoney* society defines success as owning a big house, posh car and a fat salary. Television advertising tells us we simply cannot do without a particular product. The buy-now-pay-later syndrome, with too easily acquired "little plastic friends" have caught many in the debt trap. Everything pampers to the desires of the flesh – "the lust of the flesh, the lust of the eyes and the pride of life" (1 John 2:16, New King James Bible).

The Bible calls it covetousness. How easy it is for we Christians to get caught up in this trap! We do so through the process of gradualism – being slowly influenced by the environment we live in so that, almost unconsciously, we take on its characteristics and find ourselves chasing after the same objectives as the world.

There is no doubt that God wants to bless His children, to give us abundant life, to bring healing, to loose us from Satan's bondage (Luke 4:18). But He chooses to bless us, not to satisfy ourselves (Jas. 4:3), but so that we can bless others. "Freely you have received, freely give," said Jesus. True love for God shows itself in selflessness, sacrifice and generosity – not greed.

The love of money, declares the apostle Paul, "is a root of all kinds of evil (1 Tim. 6:10)". "Godliness with contentment" is what he recommends for believers. Accumulation of possessions was not the hallmark of his life. He knew what it was to have plenty on occasions and to have little at other times. Yet in whatever circumstance he found himself, he was content (Phil. 4:11,12). His aim in life was to "know Christ and the power of his resurrection" (Phil. 3:10). God wants us to pursue His holiness (Lev. 20:7), not the so-called happiness the materialistic society we live in offers.

 **Lord, keep me from covetousness and help me to always be content in whatever material circumstances I find myself.**

 *How does James describe those who chase after riches? (Jas. 5:1–6)*

*How much influence have television advertising and mail-order catalogues got over your spending?*

 **John 17:1–26**

Sanctification is a rather old fashioned biblical word. It's not a popular word in churches today – unlike blessing, healing, wholeness, faith, miracles, signs, wonders, worship and evangelism. I have a sneaking feeling that's because it focuses on character and changing our character.

At the heart of His high priestly prayer, which we are looking at today, Jesus petitions His Father not for His disciples to be successful or prosperous in the world's terms, but that they will be kept from satisfying fleshly desires and ambitions – "Sanctify them by the truth" (v. 17). Sanctification has two aspects to it, the first "to be set apart for sacred use". God's purpose in salvation is to release us from the world's selfish ways, such as personal ambition and unbridled materialism.

Our consumer society is a continuous treadmill which panders to greed. It is a never-ending "gimmee, gimmee..." And the more we get, the more we want. The Cross spells death to all that – and we can be dead to its snares if we truly surrender to Christ there and allow God the Holy Spirit to work the necessary change in us. There is a danger, however, of allowing this to go too far one way, ending up on the path of self-denigration and denial from which the old ascetic teaching of austerity and worm theology springs. Which brings us to the second aspect of sanctification – set apart to fulfil God's will and purposes. That means that God has blessings in store for us to receive and things to achieve.

There is a danger in over-emphasing this aspect of truth, too, and become blessing-orientated. Then success and prosperity is seen almost totally in material terms – hence the rise of the so-called *prosperity gospel* in recent years. Better cars, bigger houses, higher salaries, freedom from illness...all are seen as the rights of, and even the main pursuit, of believers. It is the gospel of the consumer age, proclaiming that the earth and all its riches and resources belong to the Church. Adam, according to this gospel, forfeited these through his disobedience and negative confession, but Christians are the true inheritors of these riches through positive confession. That's a far cry from Jesus' prayer that His followers would not seek material riches, but glorify God by doing His will.

 **Lord Jesus, may true sanctification be the hallmark of my life – freedom from selfish, worldly pursuits. May I experience true blessings as I seek to follow you.**

 *What did Jesus mean by* world *in His prayer?*

*What changes do you need to make to rid yourself of the world in your life?*

 **2 Chronicles 7:12–16**

"Is it wrong for a Christian to seek material success and prosperity?" That's a question often asked. The answer is Yes – *if* we seek it for its own sake and for our sole pleasure. Pursuing it to pander to our selfish interests is pressing a self-destruct button. Today we read how God exhorts the Israelites to turn from their self-centred ways and seek His face. It's important to seek God rather than success, to seek the Giver of blessings instead of the blessings themselves, the Healer rather than healing and the Deliverer instead of deliverance.

The problem I find so often with the prosperity gospel is that it encourages us to seek God's hand rather than His face. It tells us to seek His hand of healing, protection, provision, deliverance, power...But if you want to see God's hand move, you must first seek His face.

"Surely," declared the psalmist to God, "you desire truth in the inner parts" (Ps. 51:6). All too often we try to escape God's penetrating eye that sees deep into our hearts and motives. We don't seek His face because we know that we will get a look of disapproval. Instead of His voice of encouragement we will hear a word of rebuke. Rather than his smile of acceptance we will see disappointment and grief because of our selfish, unacceptable behaviour.

So we need to seek Him with an open face and heart, allowing Him to search us deeply. Let's come to Him today, seeking His face instead of His hand. Blessing, success and prosperity will come to us if we seek Him and Him alone.

 **Lord God, I look into your face today and worship you for who you are – not what you can do.**

 *Is there anything holding you back from seeking God's face?*

*What do you think God will find when you allow Him to gaze deeply into your heart and motives?*

 **Hebrews 11:1–40**

Some Christians feel that seeking God's face rather than His hand conflicts with exercising faith. Today's passage blows this assumption apart. The roll of honour in God's hall of fame shows that these saints demonstrated their trust in God by exercising faith. There's a teaching around today that gives us the impression that faith should be the main activity and goal in the Christian life. It suggests that faith has some power in itself, a sort of faith in faith, simply an exercise in the power of belief and, when we exercise it, God *must* move to do our bidding – forced to do what our faith declares and demands. But this reduces God to some sort of cosmic force, governed only by certain laws or statements that we need to confess.

Faith, however, is not our ability to make God do what we want, but the vehicle through which we trust Him to do what He knows best. Jesus tells us to "Have faith in God" – not in faith (Mark 11:22). Faith must have an object – absolute confidence in God. Faith is my positive response to Him. I will act out of my confidence in Him. The more clearly I see Him, the more readily I will respond in rugged, fearless faith.

As the old hymn says, "Trust and obey, for there's no other way." There is no one who can be trusted implicitly except God himself. True faith grows out of obedience to Him through continually seeking His face. Faith is total dependency on Him. God does not answer our prayers at our dictates, but out of His sovereignty, wisdom, mercy and grace.

 Help me, Lord, to see that faith is not twisting your arm to do what I want, but trusting and obeying you in the midst of all my circumstances, because you always know what is best.

 *How much faith have you in God?*

*What did you learn during your latest real test of faith?*

**Matthew 6:24–34**

**DAY 7**

We live in a fallen, sinful world, where sickness and disease is rampant. I am, however, firmly convinced that Jesus' healing power is still available through the ministry of His people today. In Christ's atoning work on the Cross, God made provision for our physical as well as our spiritual needs. Our risen Lord is as willing to heal today as He was during His earthly ministry 2,000 years ago.

But Christianity isn't a healing cult that views God as a convenience, always on call to soothe away our bodily discomforts and attend to every illness, ache and pain. His top priority is not our physical and material wellbeing, but our spiritual health. The ultimate end of the Christian faith is not to make us deliriously happy or extravagantly prosperous, but to be holy.

Health, wealth and happiness are by-products of holiness. So personal ambition must be surrendered at the Cross. If we seek health and happiness first, it will evade us. But if we seek first the Kingdom of God and His righteousness, then all the other things will be added as well.

It's time to get our priorities right.

 **Thank you, dear Lord, for every blessing you have brought to my life. I rejoice in your goodness and mercy to me.**

---

### FOR GROUP DISCUSSION

- Is it right for Christians to be poor?
- Does being poor or sick indicate a lack of faith in God?
- Is it right for Christians to be rich?
- Can we claim and demand things from God?
- What is the difference between humility and denigration?
- What would you define as true prosperity and success?

---

### Suggested further reading

*Born to Shop* Mike Starkey (Monarch Publications).
*God's Time, God's Money* Sir Fred Catherwood (Hodder & Stoughton).

# WHEN WE FAIL

## Peter Meadows

*Peter Meadows is Communications Secretary at the Evangelical Alliance and author of* Pressure Points *(Kingsway). A member of the Spring Harvest Executive Committee, he and his wife, Rosemary, have five children.*

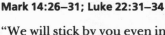

**Mark 14:26–31; Luke 22:31–34**

"We will stick by you even in the face of death." That vow was based on what the disciples *intended* to do, rather than on what they would *let God help them* to do. This is the kind of soil in which failure often grows. Within hours the vow proved to be no more than empty words. The proverb says that pride comes before a fall. But perhaps it was not pride that lay behind the emphatic declaration of allegiance that so soon led to failure.

It could have been the result of peer pressure, with each disciple determined not to lose face. Or it may have been an attempt to give a good impression to the Master whom they loved and followed.

The disciples had nothing to prove to Jesus. In carpentry terms, they were chipboard that did not require a thin layer of mahogany veneer to give the impression that they were quality wood through and through. Jesus knew them inside out – and loved them anyway.

But the end result was to set goals well outside their own ability to achieve. They were guaranteeing failure by putting the finishing tape far beyond their reach – and trusting only in themselves to get there.

 **Heavenly Father, please help me to really understand that you love me as I am. Help me to rely on you and not just on myself.**

*When did you last fail through doing or trying to do something in your own strength rather than allow God to do it through you?*

*How much does peer pressure affect you?*

 **Mark 14:32–34; John 11:17–37**

Examination results disappoint, relationships disintegrate, promises are broken, well-intentioned commitments are not kept...These and other shortcomings bring their traumas. Emotional distress readily sweeps over us. The pain from experiencing personal failure can be deep and penetrating.

There are times when failure is not failure at all. Times when we may *feel* like a failure, but do not, in fact, deserve to wear the label. Such is the pace and pressure of life that we find ourselves emotionally overrun by all that is being thrown at us. Our ability to cope runs out of road. A sense of failure engulfs us as we believe we ought to be able to keep our emotions under control.

In the garden of Gethsemane, Jesus shared in that experience. Most of us picture Him as being thoroughly British in that He always faced every difficulty with a stiff upper lip. The Bible paints a different picture. We read that "he began to be deeply distressed and troubled" and, in His own words, "overwhelmed with sorrow." This teaches us that our emotions are a gift from God. We are even commanded in Scripture to "weep with those who weep."

To feel the pain of disappointment, bereavement or pressure is not to fail. It is so normal that it is an emotion that even Jesus shared with us.

 **Lord Jesus, thank you that I was made not only with a body and a spirit, but also with emotions – just like you. Thank you that I do not fail when I experience the emotions that have been created within me.**

 *How often have you blamed yourself for failure which, in the light of today's study, isn't failure at all?*

*Do you now feel better able to cope with the disappointments and setbacks of life?*

**14:35–42; James 4:17**

It is hard to picture a Saviour who needs the support of his close friends. But it was support Jesus asked for as He faced the prospect of the Cross. In the face of pressure, we need others just as much as Jesus did. This is why the Church is intended to be a "one another" people.

Sadly, we are often as ineffective as were Peter and his friends. We, too, fall asleep on the job! Peter's failure was in not showing practical concern. Yes, prayer is practical – to someone who needs it. His was a sin of omission. Peter knew how to do good, but just didn't take any action.

It was spiritual activity that had tired Peter out. The Passover meal celebrated with Jesus, with its hymn singing, rituals and fellowship, had drained his emotions. Peter's "heavenly" activity had left him of little earthly use.

James warns of the hypocrisy that stems from failure to do the good that we ought. Not that we are asked to take the whole world's needs as our own personal responsibility, but we are called, at least, to respond by doing good to those around us – particularly our brothers and sisters in Christ (Gal. 6:10).

 **Lord God, I am sorry for the times when I have not done the good that I know I ought to have done. Please help me to get a proper balance between worshipping you and serving others.**

 *Is there anyone who needs your prayer support right now?*

*Honestly weigh up your spiritual activity. What is the ratio between it and practical care in Jesus' name?*

**Mark 14:43–47; Exodus 20:1–17**

Don't lie and don't murder say two of the ten commandments. Judas' kiss breaks both. Such moral failure can only be described by one word: *sin*. Peter was no different. He lashed out with murderous intent at the high priest's servant. We may think that we would have done better than Judas. But are we so sure that Peter's failure was any worse than ours would have been?

Both Judas and Peter were made of the same stuff as we are. A video presentation of our inner thoughts and actions would shame us. To point to the greater sins of others does not provide a shelter from the reality of our own moral failures.

In the garden of Gethsemane we see the worst of human nature. Yet that very act of betrayal led directly to forgiveness being made possible. For all who break God's laws – Judas, Peter and ourselves – "he was pierced for our transgressions ... by his wounds we are healed" (Isa. 53:5). "The blood of Jesus ... purifies us from every sin" (1 John 1:7).

 **Thank you, Heavenly Father, that Jesus died on the Cross so that I could be fully and completely forgiven. Help me to own up to my moral failings, moment by moment, so that I can experience the closeness of your fellowship at every moment.**

 *Which are you quicker at pointing the finger at – others' sins or your own?*

*Do you really believe that Jesus can forgive you for all sin and completely cleanse you?*

**Mark 14:48–50; Luke 2:39 & 40; Matthew 13:55**

Did Jesus ever fail? To even ask the question sounds unthinkable. The problem is that we find it well nigh impossible to see failure as anything other than sin. Picture Jesus growing up in the carpenters' shop. As he learned His trade, did *every* chair and *every* ox yoke turn out perfectly *every time* right from the moment He began His apprenticeship?

The mystery is that Jesus was fully God *and* fully human. So, like us, He learned from His failures. He could look at a rejected piece of handiwork content in the knowledge that He had done His best and had learned something for next time. If we see that as sin then we are being hard taskmasters on ourselves as we learn the lessons of life.

At the point when the soldiers arrived to arrest Jesus, He had invested at least three years of His life in 12 men. Despite all He had said and done, they still did not understand. His role as Saviour of the world did not require His friends to abandon Him, but that is what happened – they failed Him. Whatever our own disappointment at failing to be faithful to the Son of God may be, at that moment in Gethsemane Jesus shared the disappointment with us.

 **Lord, thank you that you understand how it feels to fail. Please help me to understand that I learn so much more from my failures than from my successes.**

 *Do you see all failures as sin or as stepping stones?*

*What have you learned from your most recent failure?*

 **Mark 14:66–72; Acts 2:37–41**

When a child is learning to walk there is always the same significant turning point. It is when, having fallen over, they do not simply sit there feeling sorry for themselves. Instead, they pick themselves up and have another go. That experience is a key transition in the process of maturity. It is the same for each of us as we wobble down the road of life. To quote Oliver Goldsmith, the British writer, "Success consists of getting up just one more time than you fall."

Whether we have failed to reach God's standards, which is sin, or failed to reach our own standards, which isn't, it is no good wallowing in self-pity and guilt. As Winston Churchill said, "Success is never final; failure is never fatal; it is the courage to continue which counts."

Failure can be of immense value. As the cock crowed, Peter's own failure to live up to his boast of continued allegiance came home to roost. He discovered a lot about himself in the process – and went on to be one of the great Christian leaders.

Failure also has the benefit of producing character. "All sun makes a desert" runs an old Arab proverb. Failure also makes us more valuable to others. Those following in our wake who taste similar failures will more readily turn to us for help and comfort.

Heavenly Father, please help me to put my failures to work, so that I may grow in character and be more useful to you and to others.

 *Are you a wallower or a walker after you've failed?*

*How has someone else been encouraged in their Christian life from a failure of yours?*

**Matthew 14:22–33**

This is the classical illustration of failure. Or is it? After all, since when is being only up to your knees in a hundred feet of water failure? Peter had a goal and went for it. He didn't get there – but just think of what he achieved through trying! The Bible does not tell us how many steps he took, but even if it was only two, it makes him the only man in history to walk on water. Yet we write him off just because he did not get as far as he intended. We are obsessed with our shortcomings rather than rejoicing over the gains that they have made possible. What we call failure was really success.

The real failures were those who stayed in the boat – dry, safe and respectable, with a *success* label tied on them. Our churches are full of people like that. Those who will never rock the boat or take the risk of failing. No wonder we achieve so little!

When Jesus calls us to follow Him, it is to a life of risk and adventure. But remember, Peter was not sitting in the boat trying to think up some mighty way in which he could demonstrate his commitment. He heard Jesus say, "Come." His obedience led to a glorious demonstration of God-honouring failure. It is this kind of failure that we must see more of if the Church is really going to flourish in today's hostile world.

 Lord Jesus, help me to clearly hear your voice and boldly and bravely risk failure in serving you.

## FOR GROUP DISCUSSION

● How have your attitudes to personal failure and others' failure changed as a result of these last seven studies?

● Share some of the things you have have learned through failing.

● How hard do you find it to accept that failure is not always sin?

● Make a list of things that are moral failures (and need repenting of) and failures that are not sin.

● In what ways have you individually, as a group and as a church failed to show love and give support to others?

● Has your church opted for safety and respectability or does it boldly step out and risk failure in order to glorify Jesus Christ?

● What is the difference between foolishness and faith?

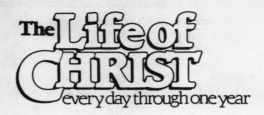

# The Life of CHRIST
### every day through one year

## Trevor Partridge,
## Rita & Neil McLaughlan

Read through the life of Jesus day by day in a
year. A chronological commentary takes you
through the New Testament records,
illuminates the events and pinpoints the
adventure and challenge of living for Jesus
today.

## Features:
- ☐ Chronological readings;
- ☐ Daily comment;
- ☐ Maps and charts;
- ☐ Ribbon marker;
- ☐ Further material for prayer,
  study and action.

## 216 pages, hardback

If you would like details of other CWR publications,
please write to:
CWR, 10 Brooklands Close, Sunbury-on-Thames,
Middx., TW16 7DX.
Readers outside the United Kingdom please contact your
National Distributor (address after title page),
or CWR UK if you do not have a National Distributor in your
country.